THE USE OF TIME

THE USE

OF

TIME

By GODFREY M. LEBHAR

57361

CHAIN STORE PUBLISHING CORP.
NEW YORK, N.Y.

THE USE OF TIME

PREFACE TO
THE THIRD EDITION

SEVERAL reasons account for this new edition. In the first place, the earlier editions are now out of print. Evidence that those editions proved of value to at least some of those who read them suggest that another edition might benefit still others if it were available.

Then, too, the original text calls for revision in at least one important particular: the normal expectancy of life today is so much greater than it was when the first chapter of the book was originally written, in 1925, that I feel obliged to direct attention to the significant change which has occurred in the interim.

The fact is that, thanks to the progress of medical science and other factors, the basis for certain observations and calculations in Chapter I no longer applies. Those calculations were based on the old "American Experience Tables of Mortality," which though valid enough at that time are now obsolete. They are retained in this edition only for reference purposes and for comparison with the far more promising life-tables which reflect our expectancy currently.

Some other revisions and additions necessitated or made possible by events since the publication of the second edition, in 1950, have also been made.

GODFREY M. LEBHAR

New York, December 7, 1957

ORIGINAL PREFACE

THE manuscript of Chapter I was written 22 years ago, in 1925. It was not published until 1936. What happened after that is explained in Chapter II.

Obviously I claim no credit for discovering the possibilities and the value of time-thrift. As the following pages disclose, no fact of life has been more generally understood and reiterated by the wise men of all ages—down to and including such modern-day philosophers as Arnold Bennett and Walter B. Pitkin.

But by the same token, no fact of life has been more consistently ignored by mankind! That is my only excuse for repeating and adding to what has already been said so much more effectively by others. If my own words on the value of time-thrift fall on deaf ears, perhaps some of my quotations from others may prove more effective.

If the circulation of these pages helps even a few of my readers to get more out of their lives it will have served its only purpose. I will be satisfied then that the time I spent in preparing them was not only not wasted but was probably the most productive time I have ever spent. For the amount of time which any single individual can employ profitably is obviously limited no matter how industrious he may be, but if by using some of my time I can induce others to use *their* time more productively then the total amount of time which may be salvaged will be limited only by the number of wise readers who undertake to salvage it!

Here is a tried and true prescription for getting the most out of life. Whether you want to take it or not is entirely up to you.

New York, October 1, 1947

PREFACE TO SECOND EDITION

THE fact that the first edition is now out of print might not in itself provide sufficient reason for printing another. But evidence that the first edition succeeded in interesting at least some of its readers in the advantages of time-thrift suggests that a new edition might render the same service for another group. In that hope, this new edition is offered.

In preparing this new edition advantage was taken of the opportunity it gave to add some new material in Chapters IV and V and to make some slight revisions and changes elsewhere.

GODFREY M. LEBHAR

New York, January 1, 1950

ACKNOWLEDGMENTS

THE quotation in Chapter IV from "Life Begins at Forty," by Walter B. Pitkin, copyrighted 1934 by the McGraw-Hill Book Company, Inc., is used with the permission of the copyright owner.

The quotations selected for the Time-Thrift Calendar, which is presented as Chapter VII, were gathered by the author over a period of years from a wide variety of sources. Among the many reference books used for comparison purposes and verification were the following:

Allibone's Prose Quotations, 1888. J. B. Lippincott Company.

Bartlett's Familiar Quotations, 11th Edition, 1938, edited by Christopher Morley. Little Brown & Co.

The Book of Old Sundials, by Hogg, 1922. T. N. Foulis, Ltd.

The Book of Sundials, by Mrs. A. Gatty, 1900. G. Bell & Sons.

Encyclopedia of Quotations, by Adam Woolever, 1898. David McKay.

Hoyt's New Cyclopedia of Practical Quotations, 1922. Funk & Wagnalls Co.

Many Thoughts of Many Minds, by Henry Southgate, 1870. Griffin & Co.

The New Dictionary of Thoughts, by Tryon Edwards, 1936. Classic Publishing Co.

The Oxford Dictionary of Quotations, 1941. Oxford University Press.

Putnam's Complete Book of Quotations, 1926. G. P. Putnam's Sons.

Ye Sundiale Booke, by Henslow, 1914. Edw. Arnold.

Wisdom of the Ages, by Mark Gilbert, 1936. Garden City Publishing Co.

CONTENTS

CHAPTER I

ONLY HOURS TO LIVE!

I HAVE just become aware that my life is now only a matter of hours!

I'm not a convicted murderer without hope of reprieve. I'm suffering from no fatal disorder. Nor am I in the hands of racketeers from whom I see no chance of escape.

The fact is that as I write these harrowing observations, I am seated at my typewriter in a New York apartment, and the calendar in front of me, which tells me it is March 13, reminds me that it is my 43rd birthday—so that my approaching end is not to be predicated on my having lived my allotted span. That I am able to discuss it in this tantalizingly slow sort of way, or even at all, in view of my statement that it is only *hours* away is due to the fact that the number of hours in question happens to be approximately 227,760!

The truth is that when I awoke this morning and realized that it was my birthday, I began to take stock of myself. For the present purpose, it matters little what the inventory showed. Suffice it to say the retrospect was not entirely ungratifying.

"So far so good," I soliloquized, "but how about the next 43 years?"

Then came the sobering query: "Is there going to be another 43 years? How long can a fellow of 43 reasonably expect to live, anyway?"

1

I remembered the Mortality Tables—which tell you the number of years a man or woman of any given age may expect to live—and grabbed for the almanac which contains all that sort of information.

I found what I wanted. The "American Experience Tables of Mortality" was rather a gloomy sort of thing to be poring over on one's birthday, but it contained just what I was looking for.*

Down the column to the left my finger travelled, stopping at intervals to allow me to digest some mighty interesting information in passing. It told me, for instance, that a child of ten may expect to live only about 48 years more—to the ripe old age of 58—despite the fact that the biblical span is three score and ten. Even a man of 21 cannot figure on more than another 41 years, or a total of 62, while a man of 33 has just about reached the half-way mark because all he may reasonably expect is 33.2 years more.

But what I was after was the age of 43, and this is what I found: "43 . . . 26." In other words, my normal expectancy of life at 43 was exactly 26 years or 227,760 hours, as I have already stated.

Just what led me to reduce my "expectancy" to hours, I don't know, but in the light of certain calculations which I proceeded to make and which I am about to discuss, that seems to have been the logical first step.

* As explained in the Preface to this Edition, these Mortality Tables reflected our expectancy in 1925. But as a result of progress made in medical science and in improved living conditions, our expectancy today is much greater than it was then. The latest tables compiled by the U. S. Public Health Service, Department of Health, Education and Welfare, are presented on page 13. Reference to those tables will reveal that whereas in 1925 the expectancy of a man of 43 was a flat 26 years, today a man of that age can expect to live 29 years more and a woman 33.9 years!

At first sight, 227,760 hours looks like quite a respectable total, but I must confess that before I figured it up, I would have guessed that the number of hours coming to me in the normal course of events would have run somewhere in the *millions!* But there it was and it couldn't be changed. The only thing to do, as I saw it, was to try to use my remaining hours to the best advantage.

Knowing that I have approximately 227,760 hours to live, I am a good deal in the position of a millionaire who, having been drawing on his bank account for years without ever having had his book balanced, has just been notified that his balance, instead of standing in the millions as he had blithely taken for granted, has been whittled down until all that he has left is a paltry $227,760.

"Gee whittaker! Where's it all gone? Thought I had enough to last me forever!" you can just hear him exclaiming. "The bank must have made a mistake!"

Of course he knows that the chances of such a mistake are slim and, like a sensible ex-millionaire, he soon takes another tack.

"Well, it's clearly time to call a halt," he decides. "I've either got to increase that balance or cut down my expenditures—or both. The least I can do at any rate is to economize until I have this thing thought out." That, at least, is about the line of reasoning he would probably follow.

What the ex-millionaire would probably do would be to adopt some sort of a budget plan, so as to keep his future expenditures within his income, instead of allowing them to eat into his capital recklessly as he had obviously been doing before.

But the millionaire with the diminished bank balance

could hardly have been more reckless with his money than I have been with my time. What his original fortune was is unimportant. The "fortune" I have gone through in these past 43 years is definitely fixed. It is exactly 376,680 hours, and that, as I realize now, is a lot of hours. The most striking thing about it though is the fact that I have gone through this "fortune" without ever stopping to figure, until today, just how much I had left.

Of course the trouble with me, and undoubtedly with most of us, is in assuming that the only thing the Expectancy Tables are good for is to enable the life insurance companies to fix premiums accurately enough to cover the risks they assume. Now I realize that these tables can be put to another important use—they can be used to tell you what your balance is in the bank of life and thus enable you to spend your remaining years to the best advantage.

There's the whole thing in a nutshell. Man's days are numbered. Why not know the number?

The ex-millionaire who had to retrench had a choice of three courses: (1) he could augment his capital; (2) he could reduce his expenditures; or (3) he could do both. Only one course, however, is open to one who wants to conserve his balance in the bank of life. He cannot augment it. All he can do is to spend it more judiciously.

And yet, strange as it may seem, there *is* a way of augmenting your balance in the bank of life, or, perhaps it would be more accurate to say, the balance *is* augmented automatically by something which is closely akin to annual interest, or a dividend! What is more remarkable and encouraging about it is that the *rate* of this interest or dividend increases from year to year as the balance in the bank grows *smaller!*

An example will make this point clear. A year ago, when I was 42, my balance stood at 234,067 hours. Today, at 43, a year later, one would expect it to be 8,760 hours less, for there are 8,760 hours in a year. That would make my present balance 225,307. As a matter of fact, however, it is 227,760, a difference of 2,453 hours in my favor. In other words, although I certainly lived 8,760 hours last year, the same as everyone else did, only 6,307 were actually deducted from my balance. My dividend for the year was thus 2,453 hours.

How substantial a factor these annual "dividends" are may be judged from the fact that at age 50 the expectancy is 183,171 hours and at age 60 it is 123,516—only 59,655 less although in ten years we actually use up 87,600 hours ($8,760 \times 10$). The "dividend" received during the decade in question thus aggregates 27,945 hours, or more than three years!

At the present moment, then, my expectancy is 26 years, or 227,760 hours. That is my principal. If I get all I can out of that principal, I can let the "dividends" take care of themselves. Indeed, any plan I adopt to conserve the principal will automatically operate to conserve the interest too.

We can save money by not spending it, but we cannot help spending time. Rich or poor, monarch or slave, philosopher or dunce, saint or sinner, we all spend our time at the identical rate of 24 hours per day, day in and day out, to the end of the chapter. The only difference is in what we get out of it.

What we get out of it! There's the big problem of life. Right here and now I purpose to find out just what I am getting out of it and how hereafter I can manage to get more. With probably only 227,760 hours to go, I am going to try to get my time's worth out of every blessed one of them. I don't expect to get 61 minutes out of an hour, but I'm going to see that I get 60.

The first big item to consider, I imagine, is sleep. Roughly speaking, one-third of our lives is spent in sleep—eight hours out of every 24. As Sir Thomas Browne put it: "The brother of death extracteth a third part of our lives."

In analyzing our expenditure of time, however—and in preparing a budget for the future we must base our estimates on past performances—that rough formula hardly suffices. What is the fact? Do I sleep eight hours a day, or more, or less? Whatever the figure, is it too much or too little? Can I safely get along with less?

These are important questions. A difference of even half-an-hour a day in one's sleeping schedule would make an appreciable total in the course of a lifetime.

Looking back, I find that I have been sleeping anywhere from six and one-half to ten hours a day. How much of that is actually needed?

Just how much sleep a man needs depends, of course, upon a number of individual circumstances—his constitution, the character of his work, his personal inclination, etc. There is no general rule—even for men engaged in the same kind of work. Some of the greatest figures in history in every branch of science and art have found it possible to get along with as few as four or five hours of sleep. Others working in precisely the same field of endeavor require anywhere from seven to nine hours.

It is not difficult, however, to ascertain with some degree of accuracy just how much sleep one actually needs. Having ascertained the safe minimum, the obvious thing to do, if one would get the most out of life, is to keep within the minimum. Any time spent in sleep beyond that which is required for bodily and mental refreshment is wanton waste. Shorten another's life five minutes and you commit murder. Sleep five minutes a day longer than you need and you shorten your own life five minutes every day you live. Ben Franklin had the right idea. "Dost thou love life?" he asked. "Then do not squander time, for that is the stuff life is made of."

Personally, I can get along nicely with six hours of sleep a day, but I have been averaging eight. Here, then, is the first big saving I can effect—two hours a day snatched bodily from the waste-heap to be put to effective use in work or exercise or recreation. Two hours a day for 26 years amounts to 18,980 hours. Converted into 24-hour days, that is equivalent to about two years and two months, but since these salvaged hours would all be waking-hours and no deduction need be made from them for sleep, this change in my daily schedule will virtually lengthen my life about two years and eleven months!

My home is approximately nine miles from my office. It takes about 45 minutes to make the trip. That is an hour and a half per day for travelling. In the crowded subway, reading is almost impossible. Certainly I could read twice as much and twice as effectively seated comfortably at my desk as I can hanging to a strap.

Here, then, is another hour and a half that could be salvaged by moving nearer to my office. At any rate, I certainly don't have to live 45 minutes away. Somewhere within 15 minutes of my place of business, there must be a suitable place to dwell. If I find it, I can credit myself with another hour per day, or, at the rate of 300 working-days per year, a saving of 300 hours per year, or 7,800 in 26 years, which is equivalent to adding another year and two months to my life.*

Before I go any further, let me make one point clear. I have no idea of increasing my available time for work by cutting into the time I now devote to exercise and play and other useful activities. On the contrary, by systematically reclaiming the hours that are now absolutely wasted, I shall have more time not only for work but for everything else as well. In this respect I shall not follow the example of the late Chief Justice White, of the United States Supreme Court, who was a particularly early riser and who explained that habit by saying that he arose with the sun so that he could complete his day's work by 9 A.M. "Then," he would add, "I have the whole day left for—work!"

Nor am I afraid that by cultivating the habit of time-thrift I shall be tempted to neglect social activities or family obligations, which involve a certain expenditure of time, of course, but without which no life is complete. Here, again, I believe my time-saving program will have just the opposite effect: it will give me more time rather than less for the things that are worth while, and by giving me more time for myself will enable me to spend more on others.

* Circumstances did not permit me to carry out that idea for some years after it occurred to me. Today, however, I am fortunate enough to be able to live only three blocks from my office, or a five minutes' walk!

In that respect, time-thrift is no different from money-thrift. As has been pointed out by students of money-thrift, thrift is not meanness but management. "Whatever thrift is, it is not avarice," declared Lord Roseberry. "Avarice is not generous; and after all, it is the thrifty people who are generous. All true generosity can proceed only from thrift, because it is no generosity to give away money which does not belong to you, as is the case with the unthrifty. And I venture to say that, of all the great philanthropists—all the great financial benefactors of their species of whom we have any record—the most generous of all must have been thrifty men."

Planning the use of one's time need no more develop crabbiness than planning the use of one's money need develop miserliness. On the contrary, the man who, by planning, has the most time to spend is obviously in a better position to devote it to whatever purpose may interest him than the aimless creature who seldom has any time he can call his own. A busy man somehow finds time for everything. A laggard never has time for anything.

To return to my time-budget and recalling that I have already added four years and one month to my life by cutting down my daily sleep schedule and eliminating the wasted hours involved in unnecessary travel—provided I can move nearer to my office—let us see what other savings may be effected.

I can think of a dozen or more everyday activities to which I am now giving more time than is actually needed. I know, for instance, that frequently I spend far more time at meals than is necessary—making due allowance for sociability and other necessary considerations. I know, too, that unnecessary time is devoted in the course of the day to small talk which benefits no one, and that even business interviews are frequently allowed to drag along inordinately because of the mutual disregard of each other's time so commonly found even among hard-headed business men.

Our working-time is undoubtedly frittered away in other ways. It may be only five minutes here and ten minutes there, but these useless expenditures of time add up. Substantial savings can undoubtedly be effected all along the line by giving due regard to their value.

What about playtime? That, too, represents a good part of life. Am I getting as much out of that as I should?

I do not underestimate the value of either exercise or recreation. They are not only valuable; they are vital. My own tastes in that direction are varied and wide.

The main trouble here is that the time we give to recreation is even less carefully managed than the time we devote to work. We are apt to play too long.

Planning the use of one's time does not mean we may not depart from the schedule upon occasion, any more than budgeting one's income and expenditures precludes an occasional unbudgeted outlay. Indeed, a carefully prepared budget provides for unexpected or emergency expenditures, or, to put it paradoxically, provision is made for expenditures not specifically provided for.

I have not attempted to figure exactly how much time I may expect to save by putting into effect the sundry economies indicated, but, conservatively, it might be put at one hour a day, or a total of 9,490 hours in 26 years. That would be equivalent to extending my life another year and five months.

Summarizing the various savings thus provided for, we have the following impressive total:

	Years	Months
Sleeping 6 hours instead of 8	2	11
Cutting down daily travel	1	2
Sundry economies	1	5
Total	5	6

Here, then, is five years and six months to be added to my life by the simple expedient of managing my time with due regard to the fact that my hours are numbered. Obviously a man who adopts a similar plan earlier in life—instead of waiting until he is 43—will reap correspondingly greater benefits.

"But," it may be asked, "what can you do with this time you reclaim? If you could actually extend your life by your budget idea, that might be worth while—if long life is a consideration—but what can you do with a multitude of odd hours and half-hours scattered through your days?"

The question is easily answered. Most of the things we get out of life require the expenditure of but a small amount of time *at* a time. The hours we save day by day become available for immediate use in whatever ways we want to spend them. Of course, if we have nothing worth while to do with our time, having more of it will be of no interest to us, any more than having money in the bank will avail us much if we have no wants to satisfy.

Then, too, to have five years and six months literally inserted into your life as you go along instead of securing an extension at the journey's end, if that were possible, gives us

AMERICAN EXPERIENCE TABLES OF MORTALITY
(As of 1925)

Age Years	Expectancy In Years	Age Years	Expectancy In Years	Age Years	Expectancy In Years
10	48.72	40	28.18	70	8.48
11	48.08	41	27.45	71	8.
12	47.45	42	26.72	72	7.55
13	46.80	43	26.	73	7.11
14	46.16	44	25.27	74	6.68
15	45.50	45	24.54	75	6.27
16	44.85	46	23.81	76	5.88
17	44.19	47	23.08	77	5.49
18	43.53	48	22.36	78	5.11
19	42.87	49	21.63	79	4.74
20	42.20	50	20.91	80	4.39
21	41.53	51	20.20	81	4.05
22	40.85	52	19.49	82	3.71
23	40.17	53	18.79	83	3.39
24	39.49	54	18.09	84	3.08
25	38.81	55	17.40	85	2.77
26	38.12	56	16.72	86	2.47
27	37.43	57	16.05	87	2.18
28	36.73	58	15.39	88	1.91
29	36.03	59	14.74	89	1.66
30	35.33	60	14.10	90	1.42
31	34.63	61	13.47	91	1.19
32	33.93	62	12.86	92	.98
33	33.21	63	12.26	93	.80
34	32.50	64	11.67	94	.64
35	31.78	65	11.10	95	.50
36	31.07	66	10.54		
37	30.35	67	10.		
38	29.62	68	9.47		
39	28.90	69	8.97		

The difference between these tables and those on the opposite page reflects the increase in longevity resulting from the progress of medical science, improved standards of living and other factors which have occurred in the past 35 years.

EXPECTATION OF LIFE, 1955
By Race and Sex

Age	Expectation in Years				Age	Expectation in Years			
Years	White		Nonwhite		Years	White		Nonwhite	
	Male	Female	Male	Female		Male	Female	Male	Female
0	67.3	73.6	61.2	65.9	37	34.4	39.5	31.0	34.5
1	68.2	74.2	63.2	67.5	38	33.5	38.6	30.2	33.6
2	67.3	73.2	62.4	66.7	39	32.6	37.6	29.4	32.8
3	66.4	72.3	61.6	65.8	40	31.7	36.7	28.6	32.0
4	65.5	71.4	60.6	64.9	41	30.8	35.8	27.9	31.1
5	64.5	70.4	59.7	64.0	42	29.9	34.8	27.1	30.3
6	63.5	69.5	58.7	63.1	43	29.0	33.9	26.3	29.5
7	62.5	68.5	57.8	62.1	44	28.2	33.0	25.5	28.7
8	61.5	67.6	56.8	61.1	45	27.3	32.1	24.8	27.9
9	60.6	66.6	55.9	60.2	46	26.5	31.2	24.1	27.2
10	59.6	65.6	54.9	59.2	47	25.6	30.3	23.4	26.4
11	58.7	64.6	53.9	58.2	48	24.8	29.5	22.7	25.7
12	57.7	63.6	53.0	57.2	49	24.0	28.6	22.0	25.0
13	56.7	62.7	52.0	56.2	50	23.2	27.7	21.3	24.3
14	55.8	61.7	51.0	55.3	51	22.4	26.8	20.6	23.6
15	54.8	60.7	50.1	54.3	52	21.6	25.9	19.9	22.9
16	53.8	59.7	49.2	53.4	53	20.9	25.1	19.3	22.3
17	52.9	58.7	48.2	52.4	54	20.1	24.2	18.7	21.6
18	51.9	57.7	47.3	51.5	55	19.4	23.4	18.1	21.0
19	51.0	56.8	46.4	50.5	56	18.7	22.5	17.5	20.4
20	50.1	55.8	45.5	49.6	57	18.0	21.7	17.0	19.8
21	49.3	54.9	44.7	48.7	58	17.3	20.9	16.4	19.2
22	48.3	53.9	43.8	47.7	59	16.7	20.1	15.9	18.7
23	47.4	52.9	42.9	46.8	60	16.0	19.3	15.4	18.1
24	46.5	52.0	42.1	45.9	61	15.3	18.5	15.0	17.6
25	45.6	51.0	41.2	45.0	62	14.7	17.7	14.5	17.0
26	44.6	50.1	40.3	44.1	63	14.1	17.0	14.0	16.5
27	43.7	49.1	39.5	43.2	64	13.5	16.2	13.6	16.0
28	42.8	48.1	38.6	42.3	65	12.9	15.5	13.2	15.5
29	41.8	47.2	37.8	41.4	66	12.4	14.8	12.8	15.1
30	40.9	46.2	36.9	40.5	67	11.8	14.1	12.5	14.7
31	40.0	45.2	36.0	39.6	68	11.3	13.5	12.2	14.4
32	39.1	44.3	35.1	38.7	69	10.8	12.8	12.0	14.1
33	38.2	43.3	34.3	37.8	70	10.3	12.2	11.7	13.8
34	37.2	42.4	33.4	37.0	75	8.0	9.2	10.4	12.0
35	36.3	41.4	32.6	36.1	80	6.1	6.7	8.9	10.1
36	35.3	40.4	31.8	35.3	85	4.8	5.0	8.2	8.9

Sources: Metropolitan Life Insurance Company and National Office of Vital Statistics.

the additional time when we are best able to use it. It extends our youth instead of our senility.

But perhaps the best answer is that it isn't possible to extend your life *one minute* when the time comes for you to cash in, whereas you can secure all the benefits of a substantial extension by the practice of time-thrift as you go along.

Time-thrift pays as it goes. You get your dividends daily. You don't have to await the journey's end to collect. Who could ask for a fairer proposition than that?

CHAPTER II

"BUT I MUST HAVE
MY SLEEP!"

Yes, that is what a number of my friends said when they read the foregoing chapter. Circulated privately in pamphlet form, it brought many interesting comments—some expressing approval and gratitude, and some expressing, rather hotly, utter disapproval. Indeed, it was largely because of the widespread interest, both pro and con, the pamphlet aroused among the two or three hundred who received it as a Christmas card ten years ago that I decided to use some of my own salvaged time to collect the material upon which these pages are based.

"Six hours' sleep may be enough for you, but *I* need at least eight and preferably nine," wrote one of my critics. He was a man between 50 and 55 years old, who practiced law with great distinction until he was drafted to take over the direction of a large industrial company whose legal adviser he had been for years. Several others made precisely the same objection.

Well, sleepy-heads, who ever said you should not have enough sleep? Who ever asked anyone to sleep only six hours if he actually needs eight? Turn the previous pages again and find, if you can, a single word suggesting that you or anyone else should try to get along with less sleep than is actually needed. All that was said in that connection was

15

that "any time spent in sleep *beyond* that which is required for bodily and mental refreshment is wanton waste," and surely that is quite a different proposition from saying one should get along with less sleep than he needs.

How much sleep do you think you need? Eight hours? Then, for Heaven's sake, sleep eight hours. Nine hours? Then, for Heaven's sake, sleep nine hours. Ten hours? By all means sleep ten hours. But if you need only eight hours of sleep and are actually taking nine, then, without any question, you are wasting one good hour every day of your life— whether you want to do anything about it or not.

"How much more time than is necessary do we spend in sleep," observed wise Ben Franklin, "forgetting that the sleeping fox catches no poultry, and there will be sleeping enough in the grave!"

Of course, you may be getting more sleep than you need and still not want to change your habit in that respect. You may *enjoy* sleeping so much that you do not want to confine your sleep to what you actually need "for bodily and mental refreshment." Well, if that is the way you feel, there is nothing in the world to compel you to change your present schedule. No one is urging you to give up a single blissful moment you are now devoting to the luxury of sleep—nor, indeed, to economize your time in any of the other ways suggested in the foregoing pages. You can do exactly as you like about it. These pages were never intended for you anyway. You can stop reading them right now if you want to, and, for all anyone will care, you can go right back to bed. What follows is intended only for those who are genuinely interested in getting all they can out of their allotted span— who realize, in the words of Rousseau, that "all that time is lost which might be better employed." If you cannot do any better with your time than by sleeping it away, by all means go on sleeping.

The first question that arises, then, is how much sleep does a person actually need?

A rather careful examination of the available scientific literature on this question leads to the following definite conclusions:

(1) The common belief that everyone needs a minimum of eight hours' sleep in 24 is baseless.

(2) The amount of sleep you need depends not a little upon the sleep habit you have developed, and that habit can be changed.

(3) Sleeping too much is apt to be just as detrimental to health and efficiency as sleeping too little.

(4) While eight hours of sleep is the *average* adult requirement it is not a *universal* requirement.

(5) Most people could get along very nicely with less sleep than they are actually taking.

Before referring to the authorities upon whose studies these conclusions are based, it may be well to present what has been said on the other side.

Thus, Edwin F. Bowers, M.D., in *Sleeping for Health,* 1919, maintains that you *cannot* sleep too much. In support of that proposition he quotes Dr. Richard C. Cabot, of the Massachusetts General Hospital, as saying: "The sleep one needs is all one can possibly soak into one's system within 24 hours!"

Dr. Bowers feels with Dr. Cabot that we need all the sleep we can get. He declares that we need have no fear of getting too much for "when we have had enough, we will wake up." He concludes that "on the average, most healthy persons require about nine hours' sleep in order to be thoroughly recuperated. Women should have half an hour or an hour more than men of the same age. But this is ordinarily a matter of the individual's power to recuperate, which depends largely upon the depth of sleep."

The main trouble with this viewpoint is that it is just a viewpoint—with nothing to support it. It rests entirely on the lazy assumption that we must need all the sleep we get because if we did not need it we would wake up. Such a theory sounds plausible enough but it takes too much for granted.

It assumes that it is always best to let nature have her own way—an assumption which is quite contrary to our everyday experiences. In a thousand different ways we are constantly bending nature to our needs. Civilization itself is the best answer to the contention that nature knows what is best for us. But for man's subjugation of natural forces and instincts, we would all still be cave men.

Is it always best to let nature take her course? Then why did you shave this morning? Why did you have your hair cut last week? Why are we constantly destroying what nature intended to grow, and preserving what nature seems bent on destroying?

No, nature may provide the raw material, but it is up to man to convert it into something more useful under civilized conditions. Nature provides timber, man lumber. Nature provides the sea, man the ships. Nature provides the air, man the plane. Nature provides food, man cooks it. And so, without extending the list ad infinitum, why should we assume that because nature provides sleep, man should not use an alarm clock?

It is no answer to say that when man turns timber into lumber he is utilizing nature rather than thwarting her— that the use of the axe to fell the tree simply brings into play the natural law of gravitation—for we can justify the use of the alarm clock in the same way. Setting the alarm clock at night to wake us up in the morning at a given hour is merely using one natural phenomenon to overcome another—employing *sound* to end *sleep* just as we use an axe to end the life of a tree and give us lumber.

The claim that we need all the sleep we can get is not only offered without supporting evidence, but, as we shall see, is fully refuted by proof to the opposite effect—that too much sleep is positively harmful.

But before passing on to that phase of the subject, reference should be made to experiments undertaken by scientists to find out just what happens when a person gets *too little sleep*.

For the purpose of such studies, men have gone without sleep for 24 hours, 48 hours, 72 hours and even longer periods, and the physical and mental effects have been measured by elaborate apparatus.

Such experiments show, as might be expected, that an excessive loss of sleep reduces mental alertness. Of course, anyone who has stayed up all night playing poker, or who has gone without his regular night's sleep for any other reason knows that, in a general way. As it is commonly put, you cannot "burn the candle at both ends" without paying for it. But science is not satisfied with knowing things in a *general* way, and so these experiments were made to prove just how much we have to pay for loss of sleep and in what kind of currency.

No doubt these scientific studies have great value in certain realms, but they have very little bearing on the question with which we are concerned at present, for the simple reason that they relate entirely to the effects of loss of sleep for *excessive* periods. That is not our question at all. Our question is simply whether we need *all* the sleep we are now getting—whether, for instance, if we are now sleeping nine hours in 24, we could not get along just as well with eight and a half or eight. Obviously that question is not answered by proving that staying up all night is no good for us or that people who are kept awake for protracted periods in the interest of science cannot solve mental arithmetic problems as quickly or as accurately as they could when getting their normal amount of sleep.

Turning now to some of the authorities who deny that we need all the sleep we can get, what do we find?

H. Addington Bruce, in *Sleep and Sleeplessness*, 1915, refers to specific cases which suggest that "most of us sleep longer than is really necessary," and declares that he personally has no doubt that that is the case.

"It has been experimentally shown," he points out, "that even following protracted vigils a surprisingly small amount of sleep is needed to effect complete recuperation. Students of sleep are agreed, in fact, that it is the quality of the sleep that counts rather than the amount, and that certain dangers, physical and mental, attend the development of an undue 'sleep habit.' "

He quotes Marie de Manaceine for the following significant observations:

"If a man sleeps longer than the repose of consciousness and the repair of the tissues require, there will, in the first place, be an enfeeblement of consciousness from lack of exercise, and, in the second place, an adaptation of the vessels to an abnormal state to the detriment of the functional circulation. Consequently we may have ground to apprehend trouble in the respiratory exchange and an overproduction of carbonic acid—not a matter of indifference to the organism, which may sooner or later be injured thereby.

"Only after the completion of growth, at the age of 19 or 20, can the duration of sleep be safely brought as low as 6 or 8 hours a day. Those who have reached middle age, the age at which consciousness and other psychic faculties have attained the zenith of their development, may content themselves with even less. On the whole it may be said that eight hours is, on the average, the amount which adults may most wisely devote to sleep."

Right here, it might be well to point out the danger of overlooking the significance of the phrase "on the average." The fact that eight hours is the amount of sleep which adults require "on the average," does *not* mean that you individually need so much, or, on the other hand, that you may not need considerably more. No doubt the manufacturers of men's hats can tell you quite accurately what is the average size hat worn by men, but that does not mean that a hat of that size will fit *you*. It *may* fit you perfectly but, on the other hand, it may be much too big or much too small. Thus, while the *average* man may need eight hours of sleep, do not jump to the conclusion that that is what *you* need.

On this point, Dr. Norman Bridges, in "Truths about Sleep," which appeared in the *Journal of the American Medical Association,* September 1, 1906, declares that many facts prove "the contention that much less than the classical eight hours of sleep will do. It is notorious that many eminent men of history have slept little, and I think hardly one who can be called an intellectual giant has been accustomed to a great amount of sleep.

"The body should probably, with an active life, rest about one-third of the time, but it is not necessary that the brain should be unconscious in sleep all this while. Perhaps no one sleeps too much but we have had surely an extreme estimate of the amount of sleep which it is indispensable that a rested body should have.

"No one knows the exact amount of sleep that in our social zone is physiological for the man, woman and child of the present century with the varying orders of enlightenment and manifold grades of work and play."

Prof. Nathaniel Kleitman, of the University of Chicago, who, according to Lawrence Lader, in *This Week Magazine,* June 15, 1947, "knows more about sleep than anyone else in the world," believes that most of the common notions about sleep are wrong. Among them he includes the notion that "you must get eight hours' sleep a night." He says that is wrong because exhaustive experiments have proved that no two people need the same amount of sleep. "One may need nine hours," he declares; "the next can get along on five."

That sleep is a habit which is largely subject to our individual control is the pertinent suggestion made by Jerome

W. Ephraim, in *Take Care of Yourself,* a recent "debunking" book which, incidentally, is constructive rather than destructive.

Pointing out the sharp distinction between the sleep habits of man and the animals lower in the evolutionary scale, he declares that man "has developed a diurnal, more or less artificial, habit of sleeping for one long period every twenty-four hours. That habit is artificial, however, only in the sense that it is not inborn but acquired. In the language of behaviorists, it is a 'conditional reflex,' in short, a habit growing out of the repetition of identical acts in a more or less identical manner.

"It is comparable in some respects to eating. Custom, not nature, has ordained three meals a day; nevertheless habit is so strong that if we go without a single meal, we feel uncomfortable, though the system may not need any food whatsoever. Reconditioning can establish quite different eating habits and the same applies to sleep."

This author, too, contends that "while eight continual hours of sleep may be desirable for an average mature adult, life can be sustained amply on less than half this period. Darwin, Franklin, Napoleon, Frederick the Great, Horace and Virgil are among the famous insomniacs of history, and insomnia does not appear to have affected their mentality or their health."

Probably the truth of the whole matter is best summed up in the following paragraph from the work in question:

"The average mature person probably feels best, physically and mentally, after about eight hours' sleep daily, but no law of nature decrees this. Many get along quite well on less, and the supposed bad effect of losing sleep is often greatly exaggerated. Actually very few hours of sleep are needed to maintain life; the rest are a luxury."

At its annual meeting in 1954, the British Medical Association gave some attention to the subject of sleep and sleeplessness. Sir Geoffrey Jefferson of Manchester, whom *Time,* in its issue of July 19, 1954, referred to as one of the world's top brain surgeons, in discussing various angles of the subject, declared "there is no optimum period that each individual should sleep each night," thus disposing of the popular notion in favor of eight hours. "The traditional eight hours is a baseless fetish," *Time* reported him as having declared, adding "there is no physiological reason why the sleep must be taken in one shift without interruption."

Macdonald Critchley, of London, a neurologist who spoke at the same meeting, is reported as having made the significant observation that "sleeping little matters little. What does matter is the anxiety it produces." Certainly if one *deliberately* changes his sleep habit so as to keep it to a desirable minimum he will suffer no anxiety and, in the view of the neurologist quoted, the fact that he sleeps less than he did before won't matter.

Of course the fact that Darwin and Franklin and Frederick the Great as well as many other distinguished characters seem to have done pretty well on very little sleep does not mean that you can do the same. On the other hand, the fact that you are not a Darwin or a Franklin or a Frederick the Great does not mean that you necessarily need more sleep than they were in the habit of taking. Maybe you do and maybe you don't. Maybe you need the *average* eight hours, and maybe you need more, but, by the same token, maybe you could get along comfortably on considerably less.

The only way to find out is to *experiment*. If you are now sleeping nine hours a day, why not find out whether you can get along just as well with eight? If you are now getting eight, why not see whether seven and a half or even seven won't satisfy you as well—not, perhaps, the first time you try it but after you have kept at it for a week or two?

The reason most people recoil at the mere thought of cutting their sleep is that they are the victims of muddy thinking. They remember the times when they have stayed up, on special occasions, until "all hours of the night," and how heavily they paid for it the next day, and they jump to the conclusion that nothing less than the amount of sleep they have been regularly getting can possibly satisfy them.

But that, of course, is quite illogical. The fact that they feel so bad the day following "a big night" does not prove at all that they need their regular eight hours or nine hours of sleep, as the case may be. It proves only that five or six hours is not enough when you are in the habit of getting eight or nine. Naturally you cannot stray so far from your regular habit without feeling it, but that is not to say that you cannot *change* your habit moderately without ill effect. Departing from a habit is one thing; changing a habit is quite another.

But, some will ask, suppose we could get along comfortably with less sleep than we are now enjoying, why should we?

Well, that question brings up so many other things that more than one chapter will be required to answer it.

CHAPTER III

THE VALUE OF TIME

O F WHAT value is an extra hour a day? What would you do with it if you had it?

The answer depends, of course, upon what life itself means to you—upon what you are doing now with the time you have.

Obviously, if your life were more or less aimless, as unfortunately the lives of so many of us are, having more time at your disposal would be of little or no advantage to you. It would probably be a disadvantage to those unfortunates to whom life is merely something to be endured from day to day, without aims, plans or hopes for themselves or for anyone else. An extra hour a day for them would be just that much more of boredom and futility.

But if, on the other hand, as your reading of these pages indicates, life means far more than that to you, if you are seriously interested in getting all you can out of it, if you have a long list of things you want to do, or to see, or to have or to be, then an extra hour a day for the rest of your life is just about the most precious and useful gift you could ever hope to receive.

If you are still young and may, therefore, reasonably expect to live for many years, the added hour a day would, as has been previously pointed out, be equivalent to many extra years in the course of your lifetime. But the older you are the more important it is to stretch your days as much as you can if you want to achieve as much as possible in the time which lies ahead of you.

Managing your time so as to get more out of it obviously presents certain problems. It means changing certain of your habits, subjecting yourself to certain inconveniences, especially at first, and curtailing or foregoing certain comforts or pleasures in which you have previously indulged.

Whether or not that is worth while—whether what you will get will be worth more than what you give up, will be for you alone to say. But if you decide that the hours you can thus salvage are worth many times the paltry price you may have to pay for them, you will be lining yourself up with some of the wisest men who ever lived.

But don't expect everybody to agree with you or to laud your time-management plans. On the contrary, probably the majority of your friends will think you are making a mistake and will offer you plenty of arguments to prove the folly of your course. "The sluggard is wiser in his own conceit," says the Proverb, "than seven men that can render a reason."

You will be told, for instance, that even a lifetime is only a flash compared with eternity, and that no matter how effectively we utilize our time, the most any of us can accomplish will still be next to nothing.

As one man put it, commenting on the views expressed in Chapter I, "Suppose we do add a few years to our lives. When we say goodbye to this world what more do most of us leave in it by reason of having slept less?"

Others will warn you against the danger of putting such a high value on time that you will squeeze all the fun out of life.

"It's the extra few minutes after the allotted hour for

lunch, and the short while we sleep after the alarm clock goes off," one of my friendly critics, a New York public school principal, writes, "that really give us as much kick as the entire meal or the whole night's sleep."

Still another, a Philadelphia real estate man, points out that he prefers the way they do things in England, having noticed while in Europe how leisurely his English friends live their lives.

"They never get down to business until 9:30 A.M., take 1½ to 2 hours for lunch usually, and Thursday nights they leave for the country until Monday," he wrote. "In the long run they seem to be just as happy and to earn just as much as those of us who attempt to get along with a minimum of sleep, recreation, time for lunch, etc. From my own experience I have learned that if I take my time and try not to work under too much pressure I accomplish more and do my work more thoroughly and accurately."

Let not these or similar discouraging observations, however sincere, change your own views as to the value of time or your determination to put all the time you can reasonably command to the best possible use.

Whether sincere or not, these arguments can be readily answered. In most cases they represent nothing more than a defensive attitude on the part of those who make no serious effort to manage their own time effectively and cannot understand why you should want to manage yours.

Let us take up some of the more common objections briefly, one by one:

OBJECTION 1: Life is so short at best, the most we can hope to accomplish is zero even if we employ every possible moment to the best advantage.

This philosophy of futility is as false as it is demoralizing.

The truth is that many of the blessings we enjoy today are the fruit of the labors of scientists and inventors, poets and artists, musicians and writers, philosophers and statesmen, teachers and preachers, industrialists and merchants, as well as myriads of day-laborers and other manual workers, who, fortunately for us, believed in no such defeatist philosophy —who devoted their lives, however short, and their efforts, however humble, to the pursuit of worthy objectives, just causes and simple honest toil. They did not stop to figure out how much or how little posterity might benefit from their efforts. They believed, with Benjamin Harrison, twenty-third president of the United States, that "it is not the length of the step, but the direction which counts." They just did their best in the time they had, and human progress testifies that collectively they had time enough.

True enough, only a comparative few of us are destined to contribute anything of outstanding importance in itself to the world at large, but even the humblest of us can and does every day contribute much of importance to himself and to those about him.

You may never win a Nobel or a Pulitzer prize nor earn the Congressional Medal of Honor, but you can win what, in its way, is as great a prize as any of them—the gratification which comes from knowing that you have put to the very best use the resources of time and ability at your command. After all, the greatest benefactor mankind ever had, whoever he may have been, never did *more* than that. Those who criticize you for trying to do *your* best, confess their own intent to do less than *theirs*.

OBJECTION 2. If you make a fetish out of time-saving, you will squeeze all the fun out of life.

The fallacy in that line of thinking is in its false assumption that the only way to gain more time for yourself is by taking it out of the time you now devote to pleasure, or to things you enjoy doing. The fact is, however, that probably most of the time you could salvage is now just *wasted*—you get neither pleasure nor profit from it. Furthermore, as has been pointed out previously, a better management of our time gives us more time for *anything* to which we want to devote it—for more work, if that's what we want, or for more "fun out of life," if that's what we want, or *both*.

True enough, if, in the interest of saving time, one were to forego that extra five minutes after lunch or that extra snooze after the alarm clock rings in the morning, one *would* be squeezing that particular kind of "fun" out of his life. But if the time thus salvaged, or an equivalent amount of it, could thereby be put to some other use of *one's own choosing* might not the net result be *more* "fun out of life" instead of less?

Obviously little can be said in favor of saving time just for the sake of saving time. Actually we cannot "save" time at all. We can arrange to use our time more productively— depending upon what we want to produce. But we can't save it. All we can do is to spend it. *How* we spend the time which is ours to spend is for each of us to decide. The main purpose of these pages is to direct attention to some of the *choices* we have.

Let us get this clear: if spending an extra five minutes in bed in the morning, or an extra hour, is your idea of the best way to spend that five minutes or that hour, by all means spend it that way. But if, on the other hand, you feel that you can get more out of life by using that five minutes, or that hour, studying Sanskrit, for instance, or weeding the garden, don't let anybody talk you out of it.

What you regard as "fun," others may regard as hopeless drudgery. If they prefer to spend more time in bed than you do, that is their privilege. Probably it won't pay you to try to convince them otherwise. Anyway it is none of your business. By the same token, however, if you happen to know a dozen different ways in which you could spend an extra five minutes in the morning more satisfactorily than by sleeping them away, why listen to the sleepy-heads?

One of our most precious freedoms is the right to spend our own time in our own way. In exercising that right, let us set *our own price* on the time we have to spend rather than be guided by the market price established by those who put little or no value on it at all.

"Be avaricious of time," said Letourneux. "Do not give any amount without receiving it in value; only allow the hours to go from you with as much regret as you would give to your gold."

"Wretched and thoughtless creatures," Addison called us, because of the way in which we spend our time. "In the only place where covetousness were a virtue," he declared, "we turn prodigals."

"Pay no moment but in purchase of its worth," said the poet Young. "And what's it worth?" he added. "Ask death-beds: they can tell!"

From one death-bed at least, that of Queen Elizabeth I, came the answer: "All my possessions for a moment of time!"

Dr. Johnson summed it all up when he said:

"That part of our time which we can spend wholly at our own choice is very small. Of the few moments which are left in our disposal, we should be so frugal as to let none of them slip from us without some equivalent."

OBJECTION 3. The leisurely life of the English is better than ours. Why hurry? You can get more work done —and better—by taking your time than you can by working under pressure.

This objection really answers itself. For if you can accomplish more and get better results by proceeding leisurely than by hurrying, who would suggest any other course? To get along with a minimum of sleep, recreation, time for lunch, etc., with no compensation for such sacrifices would hardly be recommended by anyone—certainly not by me. That would be "saving" time just for the sake of saving time, which, as we have already said, would be footless.

But if, on the other hand, by the better management of your time you can accomplish more in your chosen field of work or can gain more leisure, or *both*, why then not make the necessary adjustment?

What such critics really have in the back of their heads when they declare their preference for the English version of leisurely living is the natural aversion we *all* feel to being *regimented*. They want to do what they like when they like it. They do not want to be *told* either what to do or when to do it. And they have a fixed notion that marshalling your time according to any kind of plan is *dictation* even though it be self-imposed.

"It is bad enough," they say, "to have to rush a meal,

shorten a nap, put up a book or suspend some other inno-
cent pleasure or activity on occasion, as when you have to
make a train or keep some important engagement. But to
bring such inconveniences on yourself repeatedly day after
day through a ridiculous, self-imposed time-schedule which
puts a definite limit on everything you do, that is unthink-
able!"

And so, indeed, it should be. No matter how highly one
values time or how firmly one resolves not to waste it, it
would be a mistake to stick to a time-schedule too rigidly. To
live with a stop-watch in your hand would be to make yourself a slave of time instead of its master. Then, too, circumstances, if not personal inclination, will sometimes suggest
or require that more—or less—than the usual time be given
to a particular activity. Prudent time-management no more
requires strict adherence to the schedule in such cases than
prudent navigation requires a ship's captain to stick to his
regular course in the face of conditions which suggest a
different one.

But to go to the other extreme, as so many people do, paying little heed, or none whatever, to the passage of time, is
to be master of your time only for the purpose of throwing
it away. It is the difference between going to sea in a helm-
less boat without a chart and with no destination except that
which wind and tide may improvise, and embarking on a
ship completely under your control and steering it for a port
you have decided to make.

Certainly time-management does involve a certain amount
of self-imposed dictation. A better name for it is self-control.
It is true you cannot control your time without controlling
yourself. But if to exercise self-control is to become your

own slave, it is consoling to reflect that it also makes you your own master.

Can those who are heedless of time say as much?

OBJECTION 4. The life expectancy tables give only the *average* expectancy of life, and nobody can tell, therefore, whether he *individually* will make the average, exceed it or fall short of it. Therefore budgeting your time on the basis of life expectancy may be proceeding on a false basis.

"One cannot calculate from the behavior of aggregates what the behavior of any one individual component of the aggregate will be," was the way an English lawyer worded this objection. "The aggregate takes the average of thousands or millions of individuals," he added, "but probably not one of those individuals will come up to the average. They each will live longer or shorter (as the case may be) than the average. So that it is still true that no one can tell when will be the day of his death."

Of course it is not only true but fortunate that we cannot foretell just how long we will live. But that fact has no bearing on anything I have said regarding the benefits of time-thrift or the ways of realizing them.

The life expectancy tables *do* tell us the *probable* length of our lives based upon our present age, and that is *all* we need to ask of them. Just *because* we cannot tell accurately just how long we are going to live, common sense suggests that we use *probability*, which *is* available to us, as a substitute for *certainty*, which isn't.

Every business man knows that the budgets used both in business and in government are based entirely on *expected* revenue and *expected* expenditures. In business we can never tell just what our total sales will be nor can we always manage to keep our expenditures within predetermined limits, but our *estimates* of future sales and expenses do enable us to set up certain standards by which to control our expenditures.

We can do the same thing with our time if we think the effort worth while. If we live longer than we expected to when we started to practice time-thrift, we shall not only have gotten more out of the years we expected to live, but the additional years will also have proven more fruitful. If, on the other hand, we don't achieve the "average" we expected, we should be all the more thankful that we got as much as possible out of the years vouchsafed to us.

All through the ages, the greatest thinkers and writers have declared without reservation that the most precious thing any of us can possess is time, and they have been shocked by the careless, indifferent, reckless way in which we have always spent it. To pick only a few selections from the thousands on the same ageless theme:

"He only is rich who owns the day," said Emerson. "There is no king, rich man, fairy or demon who possesses such power as that." That is why, he said on another occasion, a man is measured by "his apprehension of a Day."

Seneca pointed out that we are always complaining that our days are few, and acting as though there would be no end of them.

"It would be a hard government that should tax its people one-tenth part of their time, to be employed in its service," said Ben Franklin, "but idleness taxes many of us much more."

Arnold Bennett, in his inspiring message: *How to Live on Twenty-four Hours a Day,* points out that: "You wake up in the morning, and, lo! your purse is magically filled with twenty-four hours of the manufactured tissue of the universe of your life! It is yours! It is the most precious of possessions."

How we sometimes fail to take advantage of some of those twenty-four magic hours is suggested by those famous lines of Horace Mann.

"Lost, yesterday, somewhere between sunrise and sunset, two golden hours, each set with sixty diamond minutes. No reward is offered, for they are gone forever."

"The time of life is short; to spend that shortness basely, 'twere too long," said Shakespeare.

"Nothing is more precious than time and those who misspend it are the greatest of prodigals," said Theophrastus.

"What a folly," said John Howe, "to dread the thought of throwing life away at once, and yet have no regard to throwing it away by parcels and piecemeal."

According to Longfellow, "Time is the life of the soul."

"What I cannot forgive in anybody," said Lord Chesterfield in one of his famous letters to his son, "is doing nothing at all with a thing so precious as time, and so irrecoverable when lost."

Robert Montgomery declared that there are no fragments as precious as those of time, and yet "none are so heedlessly lost by people who cannot make a moment, and yet can waste years."

These are certainly eternal truths. Whether we heed them or ignore them is, as it always has been, for us alone to decide. But in the light of the authority behind them and the logic upon which they rest, are they not at least entitled to everyone's serious consideration?

CHAPTER IV

ARE YOU TOO OLD?

Some of you who read these pages and who may agree in a general way that time is too valuable to be spent needlessly, may nevertheless feel that, as far as you are concerned, it is now *too late* to do anything about it.

"If I had followed such a plan when I was young," you may say, "I might have gained much from the extra time I would have had at my disposal, but now it's too late. I'm too old to derive much benefit from time-thrift now."

Make no such mistake. It will never be too late to spend your time more wisely as long as you have any time to spend at all. Indeed, the less time you figure you have left, the more you may profit, relatively speaking, by using it carefully.

Very late in life, Lacydes, an ancient philosopher, took up the study of geometry. "At your age, is it a time to be learning?" someone is reported to have asked him. "If it is not," he replied, "when will it be?"

That, of course, is the proper spirit, and history records that many men have done some of their *best* work at a time when, by some people's standards, they would be "too old" to do anything at all.

"Nothing is too late, till the tired heart shall cease to palpitate," said Longfellow, in *Morituri Salutamus,* the inspiring class-poem he wrote to celebrate the 50th anniversary

of his Class of 1825 at Bowdoin College. He himself was
then 68 years old.

Some of the examples he gave in that poem are worth
repeating:

"Cato learned Greek at eighty; Sophocles
Wrote his grand Oedipus, and Simonides
Bore off the prize of verse from his compeers,
When each had numbered more than fourscore years.
And Theophrastus, at fourscore and ten,
Had but begun his Characters of Men.
Chaucer, at Woodstock with the nightingales,
At sixty wrote the Canterbury Tales;
Goethe at Weimar, toiling to the last,
Completed Faust when eighty years were past."

Longfellow realized that these were "exceptions," but
declared that nevertheless

". . . they show
How far the gulf stream of our youth may flow
Into the arctic regions of our lives,
Where little else than life itself survives."

Naturally we are unlikely to be able to achieve in our later
years tasks which were beyond our talent or skill when we
were younger, but as Longfellow pointed out in the closing
lines of his class-poem: "Even the oldest tree some fruit may
bear," and although we may not be able to write Greek
odes, we may be able to do something else, "would we but
begin. For age is opportunity no less than youth itself,
though in another dress."

In his famous book *Life Begins at Forty,* **Prof. Walter B. Pitkin** gives many additional examples.

"Handel wrote *The Messiah* when fifty-six," he points out, "and Bach the *St. Matthew Passion* at forty-four. Haydn's best works all came after fifty, and his *Creation* was done at sixty-seven.

"Beethoven improved with every passing year; his most wonderful melodies came between forty-five and fifty-seven. Wagner's *Tristan und Isolde* came at forty-six and *Parsifal* at sixty-nine.

"In painting, Leonardo did Mona Lisa at fifty-four, while Rembrandt's five or six greatest canvases were conjured after fifty. Frans Hals did some of his loveliest things after seventy, and Michelangelo's most tremendous conceptions were projected into paint between his fifty-ninth and eighty-ninth years. Up to his thirty-seventh year that supreme artist Goya painted nothing of consequence, according to his biographers. Then came spasms of ill-health and a prodigious outburst of creative genius which steadily improved through his forties, then through his fifties, and then through his sixties, and did not deteriorate much until well in his seventies. At seventy-two he etched thirty-three extraordinary plates depicting scenes in the bull-ring and painted, besides these, a score of portraits.

"Thus," commented the professor, "in almost every major field of endeavor the same congregation of elders confronts you."

The fact that many of the greatest creative geniuses in all fields have not only continued to produce despite their advancing years but have actually improved their output the older they got would seem to provide an effective answer to those who think that time-thrift is for the young only. If it be true that the older you get the better work you can turn out, is it not even more important to get the most out of your later and better years than to use your earlier years to the best advantage?

In this connection Prof. Pitkin's book cannot be recommended too highly to those of you for whom, according to his scientifically-based theory, life is about to begin.

The professor concurs wholeheartedly with those who, like Arnold Bennett, place a high value on time and believe that it should be budgeted. "Time is the inmost stuff of life itself," he declares, quoting with approval a writer who had observed that the wise spending of time is more important than the wise spending of money.

In developing his thesis that life begins at forty, Prof. Pitkin is quick to point out that that does not, of course, apply to. our physical energies, which he readily admits pass their peak usually before we attain that age. Nor does he contend that life begins at forty for everybody. He excludes fools. The Pitkin theory is that life begins at forty only for those who have brains enough to adjust their activities to their physical and mental energies.

"After forty, sensible people lead the Simplified Life," he declares, explaining that the simplified life is "one from which all striving that does not further self-realization has been skillfully purged. The indispensables receive the full force of one's energies. Not one mouse power is frittered away on the superfluous."

His moral is that "by nothing more than self-analysis and intelligent experiment anybody reaching forty can learn to live more abundantly through adjusting work and play to the natural flow of energies."

An important point Prof. Pitkin makes is that everything we do, whether in the name of pleasure or fun or as part of what we regard as work or duty, taxes our energies, and before we do it, we ought to ask ourselves: "Can we afford it? Is there not something else to do that, in the long run, perhaps tomorrow, perhaps five years hence, will yield higher satisfaction?"

Do you still think it is *too late* for you to be getting more satisfaction out of your time and energies than you are now getting?

Dr. Thomas Tapper didn't think so at the age of 65. Let me tell you the story as he told it to me several years later.

An outstanding authority on music and musical education, the author of scores of works in that field as well as in many others, such as personal engineering and efficiency, Dr. Tapper served as educational director for a great business organization, the J. C. Penney Company, from 1916 to 1932. Some time during that period, knowing his interest in what he called "personal engineering" and the development of men, I gave him to read the manuscript of what appears here as Chapter I. He returned it to me in due course and was gracious enough to say he had found it "stimulating."

Later on, after he had retired from active work with the Penney Company, he kept an office at the company's headquarters on West 34th Street and came in every day from Chappaqua, N. Y., to attend to his many other interests, including the editing of a ten volume work for the University Society, issued as the *Personal Engineering Series.*

Lunching with me one day, he told me of some of the things he was working on—he was then 72 or 73 years old —and he gave me a brief outline of a typical day's activities.

"I get up at 5:30," he said, "have an early breakfast, and catch an 8:10 train for New York. It gets in at Grand Central at 9 o'clock. I use those 50 minutes on the train rereading some of the classics I haven't had a chance to look at for years. I follow the same course on my return trip. I get to Grand Central about fifteen or twenty minutes before my train leaves, using that time to read the evening paper. I find that usually I can read all I want to read of the daily news in that time, and so when I get on the train, I can begin where I left off in the morning in the particular book I am reading or studying at the time.

"I can't tell you how many important books I have read or re-read in the past few years in that way."

He started to tell me of some other phases of his everyday activities, and then suddenly interrupted himself to exclaim: "Why, *you* were the one who started me budgeting my time in this way! Don't you remember that manuscript you loaned me eight or nine years ago? Well, from that time to this, I have put the idea steadily to work, and you cannot imagine what a lot of additional satisfaction I have gotten out of life as a result!"

Of course, when you look through *Who's Who* and see what a prodigious amount of work Dr. Tapper turned out in his busy life—most of it long before he ever knew me or read the manuscript in question—it is hard to see how he could *ever* have allowed much of his time or energies to go to waste. He died February 24, 1958 at the age of 94.

But if the brochure I loaned Dr. Tapper inspired *him* to get even more value out of his well-used time might it not do the same for you, if you gave it a chance?

When George Bernard Shaw celebrated his 90th birthday, he was still following a strict daily routine, according to S. Winsten, compiler of a book of tributes from the nonagenarian's friends and admirers to celebrate the occasion.

He got up early and rarely went to bed before midnight, and "snow and rain, wind and sunshine," declared Mr. Winsten, in the *N. Y. Times Magazine* of July 21, 1946, "he goes to the shelter at the bottom of his garden to work. One could almost imagine him clocking in, so regular is he; and there, intent and with a smile, he sits writing till lunch."

He no longer indulged in some of the strenuous pastimes for which he had been famous 40 years earlier—motorcycling at high speed, taking an early morning swim that would have tested the endurance of many an athlete, or chopping wood with all the intensity of a lumberjack, or addressing large crowds at one of London's free-speech clinics.

But, according to the authority in question, he *was,* at age ninety, working on a new play, keeping himself up to the minute by listening to regular news broadcasts and reading the newspapers and latest books, tuning in on radio concerts, and finding time, too, to spend with other people, to write letters and to plan new tasks when those on which he was then working were finished!

At age 90, George Bernard Shaw was making every minute count—perhaps even more productively than he had done 40 years earlier when, with a greater store of physical energy, he had devoted some of his time to activities which his advanced years no longer permitted. According to Winsten, "his day is very full."

Most of the examples which have been given of individuals who have achieved great things in their advanced years are cases of men and women who have merely continued the work of their earlier years. They are offered as proof that old age does not necessarily put an end to a man's usefulness.

But more significant for our present purpose, perhaps, are the cases which show not merely that old age is no barrier to effective work, but that it is possible for old people to take up entirely new activities. In other words, whether it be true or not that "you can't teach old dogs new tricks," it is certainly not true of human beings.

The fact that the ability to learn and to use our imagination stays with us at a high level all through life is well supported by numerous recent scientific studies. Some of them were referred to by Doron K. Antrim, in "Life Begins At Fifty," which appeared in *This Week,* October 17, 1948. According to Dr. W. R. Miles, of Yale University, for instance, tests he made of the faculties of a great number of people, from 10 to 89 years old, revealed the fallacy of the notion that you can really ever be too old to learn.

Summarizing the advice of psychologists and adult-education specialists, this article lists six suggestions for those who would like to make their autumn years their best, as follows:

"1. Don't drop your schooling with your sheepskin. Want to learn Spanish, piano playing, astronomy? What's to stop you? You have the learning ability, says Dr. Miles.

"2. Don't kid yourself that you have no imagination. It's there, and it can pay dividends.

"3. Keep an open mind and don't be too sensitive to criticism. At the same time, remember that to know your faults is the first step to correcting them.

"4. Never retire to a life of inactivity. There's always plenty to do.

"5. Interest yourself in other people's lives.

"6. Put up a good front at any age and keep a trim figure."

A concluding injunction in the article to "remember Grandma Moses. She discovered she could paint—now she's famous," calls for elaboration.

"Grandma Moses" is Mrs. Anna Mary Moses, of Eagle Bridge, N. Y., who at the age of 76 found it necessary to give up her hobby, fancy needlework, because of stiff fingers. Instead of saying, "well, that's that," and resigning herself to inactivity for her remaining years, the old lady decided to take up oil painting as a new hobby.

That was in 1936. Within two years she had made a name for herself, and within 12 years, according to Webb Garrison, in the *Journal of Living,* December, 1948, "she has had thirty exhibits of her work in this country and abroad. Last Christmastime, her pictures appeared on more than 8 million cards. At 88, Grandma Moses, as she is called, sells her paintings for as much as $3,000 each!"

Obviously we cannot all expect to become oil painters at age 78, or at any other age. We do not all have that particular kind of talent. But we can at least get rid of the silly notion that because we are now 50 years old, or 60, or

65, or 70, or whatever it may be, we are too old to take up anything new. It just isn't true, and you can prove it.

Of course some of you who have led active lives or are still leading them may feel that by the time you reach the age of 50 or 60 or 65 or some other arbitrary milepost, you are entitled to rest and relaxation—that instead of organizing your time so as to get the maximum done in your later years, you ought rather to be planning to ease up and do less and less as you get older.

"I've kept my nose to the grindstone pretty steadily all my life," some of you may say, "and I have had my share of gratifying achievements. Why should I stay in harness forever?"

No one suggests, of course, that you, or anybody else, should work or plan to work *one day* or *one hour* longer than you choose. All that has been said here is that if you will only give some thought to how you are going to spend your time—and follow some more or less regular plan based on the things you have decided you want to do—you will have *more time* for the things *you want most*. If work, or anything in the nature of work, is to pass completely out of your picture after you attain a certain age, having more time to devote to whatever you contemplate doing certainly won't interfere in any way with your "no work" schedule.

Is it not perfectly clear that whatever you plan to do in your remaining years, whether it be work or loafing, or what is most likely, a happy combination of the two, time-thrift is bound to make your life fuller and happier?

Too late to start? "Nothing is too late," said Longfellow, "till the tired heart shall cease to palpitate!"

CHAPTER V

ARE YOU TOO YOUNG?

IF YOU have not yet attained the advanced age of 40, but have been sufficiently interested, nevertheless, in the subject of time-thrift to have reached this point, you may feel that although the husbanding of time may be a fine thing for those whose time is running out, it really does not mean so much to you.

That is not really so. True enough, when you get to be forty or fifty, or older, you will find it mighty important to manage your time so as to get the most out of it, but why wait until then? Why not capitalize the obvious advantage which is yours of getting the maximum out of your earlier years *as well as* your later ones? If you agree that it is folly for a man of forty or older to *waste* any part of his time, why is it not equal folly for you to *waste* any part of yours? Do you think that you are so rich in time, that you have so many hundreds of thousands of hours still to live, that you can be reckless with them now, even though you may feel the necessity later on, when your balance gets lighter, to husband them?

If you have read the foregoing pages with any degree of acceptance, you know that isn't true—that none of us lives long enough at best to achieve all that we might have achieved had we used our time more thoughtfully.

Let us say that you are only 18 years old—in the very prime of youth, with all your life in front of you.

Very few boys or girls of your age are serious-minded enough to place any great value on their use of time. If they see any virtue at all in the principles of time-thrift, they see little or no reason to apply them to their own lives.

Of course a certain percentage of students and others who are taking certain courses or aiming for a definite goal find it desirable, if not essential, to follow some sort of time-schedule in order to keep up with their work.

But I suppose that very few go as far as to budget their time to any greater extent than is necessary to dispose of their home-work or whatever else it is which requires them to be time-conscious.

A man who has to catch a train or keep an appointment will usually be careful enough to allow himself enough time to make the train or the appointment, but that kind of time-consciousness is not what we have in mind at all. It implies no appreciation of the value of time in general—of the advantages of time-budgeting not merely to catch trains but to utilize *all* the time you have in the best way possible.

But suppose you are different from the average 18-year-old, and that what wise men all through the ages have said about the preciousness of time and the utter folly of wasting it, makes sense to you. Suppose you decide to make a real effort from *this day* on to get the most out of every hour you live. What do you think such a resolution would mean to you in terms of success if you stuck to it throughout your life?

Let William Ewart Gladstone, one of England's greatest statesmen, answer your question:

"Believe me when I tell you," he said, "that thrift of time will repay you in after life with a usury of profit beyond your most sanguine dreams, and that the *waste* of it will make you dwindle alike in intellectual and moral stature beyond your darkest reckonings."

And Lord Chesterfield did not think his son was too young *at eight* to appreciate the value of time. In one of his famous *Letters To His Son,* written June 25, 1740, he referred to "an Historical, Chronological and Geographical Dictionary" he was sending the boy, and said: "You will find a thousand interesting stories to divert you, when you have leisure from your studies, or your play; for one must always be doing something and never lavish away so valuable a thing as time; which if once lost, can never be regained."

In a subsequent letter, when the boy was 14, Lord Chesterfield declared:

"I hope you employ your whole time, which few people do; and that you put every moment to profit of some kind or other. I call company, walking, riding, etc., employing one's time, and upon proper occasion, very usefully; but what I cannot forgive in anybody is sauntering, and doing nothing at all, with a thing so precious as time, and so irrecoverable when lost."

The following year, in another letter, he said:

"I recommend to you to take care of the minutes; for the hours will take care of themselves. I am very sure that many people lose two or three hours a day by not taking care of the minutes. Never think any portion of time whatsoever too short to be employed; something or other may always be done with it."

Only a month later, he emphasized the same point again in the following words:

"There is nothing which I wish more that you should

know, and which fewer people do know, than the true use and value of time. It is in everybody's mouth; but in few people's practice. Every fool, who slatterns away his whole time in nothings, utters, however, some trite commonplace sentence, of which there are millions, to prove, at once, the value and the fleetness of time. The sun-dials all over Europe have some ingenious inscriptions to that effect; so that nobody squanders away their time without hearing and seeing daily how necessary it is to employ it well, and how irrecoverable it is if lost. But all these admonitions are useless where there is not a fund of good sense and reason to suggest them rather than to receive them. By the manner in which you now tell me that you employ your time, I flatter myself that you have that fund; that is the fund which will make you rich indeed. I do not mean, therefore, to give you a critical essay on the use and abuse of time; but I will only give you some hints with regard to the use of one particular period of that long time which I hope you have before you; I mean, the next two years. Remember then, that whatever knowledge you do not solidly lay the foundation of before you are eighteen, you will never be the master of while you breathe. Knowledge is a comfortable and necessary retreat and shelter for us in an advanced age; and if you do not plant it while young, it will give us no shade when we grow old. This, therefore, is your time, and your only time, for unwearied and uninterrupted application."

Finally, when the boy was 16 years old, this was what Lord Chesterfield wrote him:

"I must observe to you upon this occasion [his retirement from active business] that the uninterrupted satisfaction that I expect to find in my library will be chiefly owing to my having employed some part of my life well at your age. I wish I had employed it better, and my satisfaction would be now complete; but, however, I planted while young that degree of knowledge which is now my refuge and my shelter. Make your plantations still more extensive; they will more than pay you for your trouble.

"I do not regret the time that I passed in pleasures; they were seasonable; they were the pleasures of youth, and I enjoyed them while young. Nor do I regret the time that I have passed in business. But what I do, and ever shall regret, is the time which, while young, I lost in mere idleness, and in doing nothing. This is the common effect of the inconsideracy of youth, against which I beg you will be most carefully upon your guard. The value of moments, when cast up, is immense, if well employed; if thrown away, their loss is irrecoverable. Every moment may be put to some use, and that with more pleasure than if unemployed. Do not imagine that by the employment of time, I mean an uninterrupted application to serious studies. No; pleasures are, at proper times, both as necessary and as useful; they fashion and form you for the world; they teach you characters, and show you the human heart in the unguarded minutes. But then remember to make that use of them."

Of course you may not agree with all the advice Lord Chesterfield gave to his son in the famous series of letters, but certainly you will find nothing to quarrel with in his reiterated observations on the value of time-thrift. You *know* that time-thrift is one of the most valuable habits any one can develop, and that the sooner you develop it, the more it will obviously mean to you.

Still assuming that you are 18 now, you may reasonably

look forward to some 52 years of more or less active life according to the current expectancy table. With some 52 years of life ahead of you—455,520 hours—think what it will mean to you in terms of *effective living* and *achievement,* if you adopt right now the habit of getting the most out of each and every blessed one of them!

The fact that you cannot be *sure,* nobody can be sure, just how many years you may actually be destined to live, is no reason whatever for not adopting at once the priceless habit of time-thrift. On the contrary, whether your years are destined to be many or few, the more you get out of each of them, the more you will get out of life itself.

Dr. Colton put it this way: "No man can promise himself even fifty years of life, but any man may if he please live in the proportion of fifty years in forty: let him rise early that he may have the day before him."

This habit of early rising is so important, and at the age of 18 you have such a wonderful opportunity to capitalize it to the full, that it may be worth while to record here what others have said about it.

"The difference between rising at five and rising at seven in the morning, for the space of forty years," said Doddridge, "supposing a man to go to bed at the same hour at night, is nearly equivalent to the addition of ten years to a man's life." Apparently, he meant 10 years of *eight-hour working-days,* because that is what two hours a day of extra time for 40 years would actually yield, but what a precious addition to any man's life that would be!

And Timothy Flint, an early American author, expressed himself clearly enough when he said: "I have hardly words for the estimate I form of the sluggard, male or female, that has formed the habit of wasting the early prime of day in bed."

"He that from childhood has made rising betimes familiar to him will not waste the best part of his life in drowsiness and lying abed," said John Locke.

Wordsworth confessed that he had not made the best use of his youthful years when he said: "Multitude of hours pilfered away by what the bard who sang of the Enchanter Indolence hath called 'good natured lounging,' and behold a map of my collegiate life!"

Dr. Colton pointed out that "early rising not only gives us more life in the same number of years, but adds, likewise, to their number."

You do not have to take John Jacob Astor's formula literally, but this is what he said about early rising:

"The man who makes it the habit of his life to go to bed at nine o'clock usually gets rich and is always reliable. Of course, going to bed does not make him rich—I merely mean that such a man will in all probability be up early in the morning and do a big day's work, so his weary bones put him to bed early. Honest men work by day. It's all a matter of habit, and good habits in America make any man rich. Wealth is largely a matter of habit."

And quoting Dr. Flint again, he expressed the same general thought when he said: "Next to temperance, a quiet conscience, a cheerful mind, and active habits, I place early rising as a means of health and happiness."

To turn from the testimony of some of the sages of the past to that of one of the great men of our own day, let me tell the story of the late Chief Justice Arthur T. Vanderbilt, of the New Jersey Supreme Court, whose respect for the value of time went back to his college days and persisted all through an unusually active, successful and inspiring career.

Judge Vanderbilt was born in Newark, N. J., in 1888. He went to Wesleyan University and graduated in 1910. Then he studied law at Columbia University. He graduated in 1913, was admitted to the bar and started in practice as a lawyer. The very next year, without giving up his law practice, he started teaching law at New York University Law School and he stuck to it until 1948 when he resigned from his post as Dean of the Law School, which he had occupied for five years, only to accept the distinguished position of Chief Justice.

But the significant fact about Judge Vanderbilt's career for our purpose concerns the many extra-curricular activities he carried on simultaneously with his two main jobs as a practicing lawyer and a law professor. How could he possibly find time for all the things he undertook and achieved? Let us take a look at some of them.

Not only did he have a large and successful law practice, serving as general counsel for many important financial and industrial corporations, and acting as a director of some of them, but he was always active in local, state and national politics. From 1919 to 1947, he served not only as president of the Essex County Republican League but as the active leader of that organization's long fight for good government against powerful political bosses. What that meant in terms of time-consuming work is best described by Col. George H. Williams, who was his Assistant during his Deanship of the N. Y. U. Law School, and who recently wrote:

"There was no escape from the continual pressure, but so great was Mr. Vanderbilt's conviction of the importance of local self-government that he toiled at it for twenty-seven years even though this meant getting to his office by eight o'clock in the morning—often seven o'clock—answering correspondence and planning the work of his associates until it was time to go to court, returning from court late in the afternoon for conferences with clients and political leaders, which continued until they were disposed of, with evenings devoted largely to teaching and preparation for trial.

"I have never met a man who knew better the value of time and how to control it, or who seemed less rushed than he."

In addition to his practice, his teaching and his activity in politics, Judge Vanderbilt always played an active role in the affairs of the outstanding association in his profession, the American Bar Association. By 1937, his standing as a jurist was so high, that he was elected president of that organization, a job which he filled without giving up any of his many other activities.

In fact, the greater the prestige Judge Vanderbilt gained in his profession as he went along, the greater were the responsibilities he was asked to assume. He was in constant demand to head up special commissions and committees to draft new laws and codes or to revise existing ones.

To mention one of his most important contributions in that direction, in 1941 the Chief Justice of the U. S. Supreme Court selected him to serve as chairman of a committee to draft an entirely new set of Rules of Criminal Procedure for the Federal Courts. It was an arduous and time-consuming job, but under Judge Vanderbilt's direction it was done in five years, and the new rules went into effect in 1946. Another important assignment, which in this instance came from the War Department, was his appointment as chairman of a committee to revise the Code of Military Justice.

Another big job which fell naturally to him in addition to all the others was that of organizing the entirely new judicial system for New Jersey which was called for by the new Constitution. Judge Vanderbilt had served as chairman of the State's Judicial Council from 1930 to 1940 and was a member of the State Constitution Revision Commission in 1942-1943. When the new Constitution was adopted, he was asked not only to set up the state's new judicial system but to become the State's first Chief Justice.

Despite all these varied but contemporaneous activities, Judge Vanderbilt found time to produce several law books, either as author or editor, and he had to supervise many other publications issued by the law school faculty.

And yet he still found time apparently to dream and to plan for what may some day be regarded as his crowning achievement. He conceived for New York University a Law Center which would do for the law what Medical Centers have done for medicine. The Law Center which he envisioned and which, through his leadership, was erected in 1951, was to serve not only as a home for the N. Y. U. Law School but as the focal point for a wide range of projects and activities designed to promote the study, the development and the administration of law and justice in all its phases.

To add to the many other calls on his time, Judge Vanderbilt naturally became a chronic recipient of honorary degrees, which he had to accept in person in most instances. In the last 20 years of his life, some 20 universities conferred the honorary degree of LL.D. or D.C.L. on him—as many as four of them in a single year. In 1946, Wesleyan University, his alma mater, which had already given him an LL.D. elected him president of its Board of Trustees. And in 1948, probably one of his most highly esteemed honors came to him—the award by the American Bar Association of its coveted Gold Medal for "conspicuous service to the cause of American jurisprudence."

How did he do it? How could one man find time for the tremendous amount of work involved in all these varied activities most of which required study, research and creative thinking as well as administration and direction?

As you may have guessed, Judge Vanderbilt's secret weapon was that he made every moment of his time count. He had acquired the habit early in his youth. He himself gives credit for the formation of that habit to a book he read while he was a student at Wesleyan.

In a letter to the present author acknowledging a copy of the first edition of *The Use of Time,* he wrote:

"I want you to know how very much I enjoyed your book. You have guessed the truth about me, for I will fight for time harder than I will for most anything else. Your book should somehow or other be placed in the hands of every boy who wants to make the most of himself.

"I am wondering if you have come across a book published nearly a century ago called Todd's Student Manual. There was a chapter in it on Time that has influenced my habits more than anything else I have ever read. After forty odd years, I can still remember its main points."

The important thing, of course, is not that the Judge still

remembered the main points of the book he mentioned but that he had followed them consistently all through his rich and useful life.

The book in question was written by the Rev. John Todd in 1835, under the name 'Student's Manual." It must have had considerable circulation because several later editions were published. You can see some of them in the New York Public Library and probably in many other public libraries.

For the benefit of those who may not have access to the words of wisdom which meant so much to Judge Vanderbilt and undoubtedly to thousands of others, the following extracts are offered.

"Few ever lived to a great age, and fewer still ever became distinguished," said Dr. Todd, "who were not in the habit of early rising."

He quoted Peter the Great as saying: "I am for making my life as long as I can, and therefore sleep as little as possible." And he quoted Dr. Doddridge for the statement regarding the difference between rising at five and rising at seven, which has been previously referred to (page 52), pointing out that Dr. Doddridge himself used the time so salvaged to produce one of his principal works.

"Nothing is easier to cultivate than the habit of sleep," Dr. Todd warns, "so that the system demands, and will be deranged if the demand be denied, eight or ten hours out of the twenty-four. Physicians usually say that six hours are sufficient for all purposes of health; and were the eyes to close the moment you reach the pillow, perhaps six hours would be sufficient for the bed. But suppose you allow seven, and rigidly adhere to that number as a rule. Would you not have much more time than you now have? . . . But the waste of time is not all. The whole system is prostrated by indulging the luxury of sleep. The body and mind are both weakened by it."

Some of Dr. Todd's other observations follow:

"You neglect duties, public and private, and satisfy conscience that you have not time to fulfill them all. But the wasted hours cry out against you."

"You are in danger from any recreation which you love much; for men always give their time freely to what they love."

"A man may do a full day's work in the afternoon; but if he puts it off till that time, he will be unhappy all the morning, over-laboring in the afternoon, and sick in the evening."

"Sloth has frequently and justly been denominated the rust of the soul. The habit is easily acquired, or rather it is part of our very nature to be indolent. It grows fast by indulgence, and soon seizes upon the soul with the violence and strength of an armed man."

"The great mistake with us seems to be that we feel that we cannot do anything unless we have all our time to devote to that particular thing."

"No change, great or marked, in your general course is necessary to make new and rich acquisitions; only save every moment of time which you now throw away, and you will be able to do anything."

"Nearly all that I have ever attained, or done, out of the regular routine of my professional duties, has been by taking advantage of those odd moments which are so easily thrown away."

"There is no more effectual way of resting the mind than to have something on hand to occupy it."

"It is a prodigious thing to consider that, although, amongst all the talents which are committed to our steward-ship, time, upon several accounts, is the most precious; yet there is not any one of which the generality of men are more profuse or regardless. Nay, it is obvious to observe, that even those persons who are frugal and thrifty in everything else, are extremely prodigal of their best revenue, time; of which, as Seneca nobly says, 'it is a virtue to be coveteous.' It is amazing to think how much time may be gained by proper economy."

"At the beginning of each day, see what and how much you want to accomplish before you sleep, and then at once begin to execute your plans, suffering no time to run waste between planning and acting. At the close of the day be impartial and thorough in reviewing the day, and noting wherein you failed."

Whether or not these observations of Dr. Todd written more than a hundred years ago make as much sense to you as they did to Judge Vanderbilt when he read them as a college-student, this much is certain: agreeing with them in principle is not enough—you've got to put them to work.

Right here, let me reiterate, I do not suggest that you or anybody else should give *one minute* less to sleep than you actually *need*. How much you need you can determine easily enough by experiment. Keep a record for a few weeks of how much sleep you usually take and then start to see how much *less* you can really get along with.

You don't have to do anything drastic along these lines, but neither should you reach the conclusion too soon that you have cut your sleeping-hours as much as you could consistent with your physical needs. If you are really convinced of the important part which time-thrift can play in your life, I feel rather sure that you will see the wisdom of ending as soon as possible one of the most unforgivable wastes of time—the time spent in sleep that is not needed.

Of course, early rising, or reduced sleeping time no matter how it be achieved, is only one of the many ways in which one's time can be put to more effective use. Others have been referred to in previous chapters. The point I want to make here for the benefit of my younger readers is that whatever benefits time-thrift offers, the earlier in life you begin it, the more it will obviously mean to you.

Don't overlook the fact that time-thrift is a *habit*. It is easier to form habits when you are young than to acquire them later in life. The good habits you form now will serve you in good stead the rest of your life. The good habits you *don't* form now, you may never form.

Are you too young to give thought to this matter of time-management? Nobody who is old enough and intelligent enough to understand and concede the logic of time-thrift is too young to practice it. And a mighty good place to begin is to check up on your sleep habit. If you find that you don't really need all the sleep you are now getting, why not start *at once* to salvage those wasted hours or minutes?

The day you start really taking control of your time will in all probability turn out to have been one of the most important days in your whole life. Make a note of the date. In years to come you may feel justified in taking enough time out to celebrate its anniversary appropriately!

CHAPTER VI

TIME-MANAGEMENT
IN BUSINESS

THE MORE SUCCESSFUL a man is, whatever his vocation, the greater are the demands on his time. A leader in business or a profession naturally wants to put his abilities, knowledge and experience to maximum use, whether for his own enrichment or gratification or for the benefit of others, or both. How to find enough time to do all the things which such a man *must* do and still be able to take on more of those he would *like* to do is a universal problem for which no solution has yet been found.

Furthermore this is a problem which plagues not only the men who have already made their mark but those on the lower rungs of the ladder as well.

But although the problem defies solution, because nobody can ever find time to do everything he would like to do, the condition it presents can be greatly ameliorated. Many who say, and feel, that they haven't time to do all the things they would like to do could nevertheless do far more than they are doing by using their time more efficiently. Just because you are busy every minute of the day doesn't necessarily mean that you are using your time as productively as you could. Let it be conceded that everything you are doing is not only important but must be done and that your various activities fill every moment of your time, the fact remains that you might achieve just as much in less time by merely changing some of your ways.

Let us take, for instance, one of the most time-consuming activities in almost every busy man's daily schedule—his reading. I'm not referring to reading for amusement or relaxation, but to the indispensable kind of reading which every business or professional man must do to give him the facts upon which to base decisions or to keep him abreast of developments in the various areas in which he is particularly interested.

Have you any idea of just how much of your day your own reading takes?

If not, you'll be interested in a study the American Management Association undertook recently to find out from its members, all top-flight executives, just what their reading habits were and how much time their must-reading required.

In making its survey, the Association had no axe to grind and the executives who responded could have had no motive to give anything but accurate information. True enough, of the 996 executives queried only 213 responded, but that doesn't reduce the value of the data compiled from the responses received. Probably most of those who failed to respond were too busy reading all the stuff they have to read to cooperate in a study which might show them how they could lighten their load.

The most significant conclusion to be drawn from the survey so far as the present purpose is concerned is that the typical American executive spends at least *four hours a day* reading business reports, correspondence, books, newsletters and business magazines! And if he doesn't get through his day's accumulation by 5 o'clock, he takes the balance home in his brief-case in the hope that he may do an hour's reading before he returns to the office the next morning.

On this basis, reading takes approximately *one-half* of a busy executive's typical day at the office. Anything that can be done to lighten such a load must obviously represent a major gain in his quest for more time.

Actually a man's reading time can be cut down materially in one or more of several ways. One, obviously enough, is just not to read so much by the simple process of elimination. An analysis of what you are now reading may reveal that not everything which comes to you is worth the time you give it. Perhaps, for instance, you have been reading two or more media which overlap each other, such as two newspapers where one might be enough. Perhaps some of the stuff that is routed to you regularly is really of only minor interest to you. If you never saw it at all, or at least saw it less frequently, perhaps all useful purposes would be served.

The main thing in this connection is to recognize the wisdom of taking an immediate inventory of all the things you are now reading more or less regularly, or trying to do so, with the idea of definitely eliminating the least important of them.

Another way, for those who can utilize it, is to delegate some of your reading to someone else. Obviously your second pair of eyes must be someone who knows, or who can learn to know, the kind of things in which you are mainly interested. If all the material which now clutters your desk, or finds its way into your brief-case to be read after hours, could be intelligently screened by such an individual, the time you would save would, in most cases, be substantial.

But probably the best way of all to reduce the time you now devote to reading without missing anything that is important to you is to improve your reading technique. The fact is that unless your reading speed is above average, you are not even half as effective as you might be! In other words, thoroughly reliable studies have established that the average reader covers about 250 words a minute, whereas a good reader will do 500 or 600 words a minute and still capture as much of the sense of what he has read as a slower reader.

The important thing in this connection is that reading speed can be developed. Whatever your present reading speed may be, the chances are you can increase it substantially by taking the necessary steps. Not only have many books been written on the subject but hundreds of reading clinics have been established all over the country for the sole purpose of improving reading efficiency. The Reading Institute of New York University is just one of them, and the book "Reading Improvement for Adults," by Nila Banton Smith, Director of the Institute, is just one of the many available. It was published by Prentice-Hall, Inc., New York, in 1956, and can be recommended.

Whether you undertake to improve your reading technique by following the advice given in one of the books on the subject, or enroll for a regular course at one of the reading clinics, is for you to decide. But this much is clear: if you really want to make the most of your time and if reading now takes a goodly portion of it, improving your reading speed offers one of the most productive ways to get what you are after.

Reading must be given prime consideration because it takes up so much of a busy man's time in most cases. But many other activities may likewise be taking more time than is absolutely necessary. Ray Josephs, in his book "How to Gain an Extra Hour Every Day," lists many of them. But the first thing to do is to make up your own list of your every-day activities with the idea of working out time-saving changes.

Such a list would ordinarily include your daily correspondence, interviews and conferences with your own associates or outsiders, telephone calls, attending meetings, etc. The way you are now handling all these more or less regular features of your daily work is not necessarily the most efficient way. Compare your methods with those other busy men have found to be less time-consuming. Mr. Josephs lists many of them and you will find still others in similar books on the subject. It will pay you to explore them all, for even though the gain from a single change may be slight, the time you will save cumulatively over a period of weeks, months or years will probably be substantial.

One mistake many busy people make is to reiterate constantly that they just don't have the time to take on any additional activity. Of course, if you don't want to take on a particular activity, the fact that you are already a very busy man provides a ready excuse for turning it down. But if you use the excuse often enough, you'll soon come to believe it yourself—to your own detriment.

The fact is that in the case of time as in the case of money, how much you can afford to spend in a given direction is a relative matter. Just because something you want costs a lot of money does not necessarily mean that you *cannot* afford it. Conversely, just because something is cheap doesn't mean that you *can* afford it. It's not how much you spend, whether of money or time, that counts but what you get for what you spend.

Time-management resembles money-management in another respect. To use the terms more commonly applied to financial transactions, you can use your time as well as your money for either "a quick turn," or "for the long pull." When, for instance, you put five or ten minutes into such an operation as your morning shave, what you are looking for is "a quick turn." You know that the expenditure of those five or ten minutes will give you an immediate return in the shape of the satisfaction which comes from having performed a necessary but comforting chore. But some expenditures of time, like some investments of money, offer no such quick or so certain a return. The time you put into some projects may yield no pay-off for weeks, or months or even years. In such cases, you are working "for the long pull." Some of the greatest rewards that may come your way will be the fruit of just such long-term investments of your time.

The distinction between spending time and investing it is an important one. Unless it is recognized and kept in mind, one is apt to miss many a good opportunity for using time to the best advantage.

What Lawrence A. Appley, president of the American Management Association, had to say on this point ought to carry considerable weight. As the head of an institution devoted to promoting efficiency in industrial management, his views on this phase of time-management, are well worth quoting at length. With his permission, they are used here as he expressed them in his Association's regular bulletin, under the heading: "Time Invested vs. Time Spent."

"Recently, among the writings of Horace Mann, the great American educator," Mr. Appley wrote, "I came across a public notice which he had composed in a moment of self-criticism: 'LOST, yesterday, somewhere between sunrise and sunset, two golden hours, each set with sixty diamond minutes. No reward is offered, for they are gone forever.'

"These are the words of a man who respected the irretrievable quality of time that makes it so precious. 'Time is money' we say, though most of us realize full well that it is more than that. Like money, however, it can be spent prodigally, with nothing to show for it—'no reward offered.' Or, like money it can be used to enrich the future. This, then, is the important distinction between the *expenditure* and the *investment* of time.

"To make the analogy more specific, if an individual wants to have money to invest in order that he may receive something in return, he must make definite provision for it. He must decide to take a certain percentage of each pay check and set it aside for investment. He must do this regularly, regardless of his living expenses, debts, or other financial commitments. If his investment is sound, he receives something that he would not have received if he had spent the money. He is then in a much better position to meet current obligations and emergencies, for he has deliberately increased the value of his assets.

"Similarly, an individual can dissipate all his time on

current needs, demands, and emergencies, feeling that he has little to spare for 'investment' purposes; or he can set aside a certain amount of it for self-development. In the latter case, he is investing a specific amount of his time to increase his own abilities and thus make more effective use of the time which lies ahead of him.

"This thought recurred to me frequently during the recent opening of AMA's Management Training Course at the Hotel Astor in New York. Here was a group of executives (presidents, executive vice-presidents, heads of marketing, finance, personnel, etc.) who were devoting from one to six weeks (spread over a period of months) to increase their understanding of and competency in the performance of management responsibilities. Their studies covered the nature of management as an activity in itself, the skills and tools of management, and the means of applying them most effectively. At the completion of the first week, those in each group seemed unanimous in their belief that they would be able to do their jobs more effectively thereafter and to use time more advantageously.

"While individuals who participate in this kind of activity take time away from the performance of their regular responsibilities, they are investing it in a way that will bring them a greater return and enhance their value to their own organizations. In other words, they will ultimately receive more from the time thus spent than if they had remained on their jobs, continuously taking care of day-to-day responsibilities. They are investing time—not merely spending it.

"When an individual invests time in discussing with others, who are competent and experienced in his field, how to do his own job better, one of three results is bound to occur: He discovers that he is on the right course and moves ahead with greater confidence and less time-consuming hesitancy; he learns of a new way to do it; or thought processes are started which enable him to discover a better way for himself. The results can be in terms of a specific answer to a specific problem or in terms of a new attitude toward, or basic approach to, his over-all job.

"The instances of immediate rewards in the form of new and readily usable ideas resulting from participation in these activities are literally countless: Company presidents have completely revised their policies and procedures after hearing the experience and philosophy of another organization; individuals have brought back ideas that have meant substantial improvements in the profit positions of their companies; but more frequently and most important of all, participants have acquired a fresh approach to a familiar job, inspired by association with individuals who are facing the same problems.

"While those who are participating in this kind of activity attend willingly and appreciate the return they are receiving, there are many who do not believe in such activities or claim they cannot find the time for them. There are some 'realists' who believe it is far better to stay on the job continually than to take an occasional week here and there 'sitting in courses, conferences and meetings.' It takes courage to set aside money for investment in order to receive a greater value from money earned. It takes even more courage to set aside time for investment in order to receive a greater return from the time still available to us.

"It is encouraging to see the increasing number of

management people who possess this courage. They have enough courage even to face the doubting and cynical comments made by associates and superiors when they use their time in this way. There is no question, however, that we shall all be better for it."

The point I have tried to make in this chapter is that every activity you may be thinking of engaging in should be judged on the basis of its ultimate rather than its immediate value to you. You can follow Kipling's meaningful admonition to "fill every unforgiving minute with sixty seconds' worth of distance run," even though the pay-off may sometimes be deferred.

And for the sake of the misguided individual who may say: "I'm already carrying as great a load as I can bear, why should I try to find ways to add to it?" let me reiterate what has been said several times in earlier chapters. Better management of one's working time does not mean that the salvaged minutes or hours should necessarily be devoted to more work. By doing one's work in less time than it would otherwise take, you will have more time for whatever you want to use it for—more work, certainly, if that is where your greatest interest lies, or more leisure or after-hours activities if that is what you most need.

Some of the ways in which you could put additional time to use are covered in the following chapter.

CHAPTER VII

HOW TO USE SALVAGED TIME

MANY who agree that too much time is wasted and who would really like to put their own time to better use, do nothing about it.

Some are afraid that they would be laughed at if they started suddenly to save what everybody else spends so freely, just as we smile at those poor creatures we read about occasionally who clutter their homes with old newspapers, pieces of broken glass or other refuse which most people throw away.

Others, as has already been pointed out, feel that they have already squandered so much time that it would not help matters much to start husbanding it now—that it's too late.

But probably the most common reason for time-wasting is the feeling that the scattered scraps of time that could undoubtedly be saved if the effort were made could not be put to any practical use anyway.

The fact is that if you are really interested in managing your time to the best advantage, you *can* put the scattered fragments of salvaged time to effective use in a great variety of dividend-paying ways.

Before considering some of the specific ways in which scraps of time can be utilized, let us spend a moment or two on what would seem to be a broader problem. What would you do with your time if you didn't have to work at all—if you had reached the point where you could retire?

Under such conditions, it is logical to assume that you would plan just how you would use your new-found leisure. You would probably make a list of all the things you would like to do—that you have been wanting to do all your life—where you would travel, what you would read, whom you would visit, what recreation you would seek and, let us hope, what useful service you might be able to undertake.

Why not make up such a list right now, "making believe" that you are going to retire from active work next month?

Why? Because if you make up a pretty complete list of the things you would like to do when you retire, you will find that you can enjoy many of them *before* you retire! The more complete and detailed you make the list, the more things you will find you could do right now *if you had the time.*

There, in a general way, is the solution of the problem of what to do with the extra hours time-thrift would put at your disposal. Indeed, the real "pay-off" of time-thrift is that it enables you to enjoy *now* some of the satisfactions you would otherwise defer until that indefinite "some day" which may never come.

Obviously you will not be able to achieve as much in a few salvaged hours per day as you could if *all* your time were your own, but that is not the point. What we are concerned with now is what can be done with the hours that can be salvaged and which are within your reach. The fact that *some day* you may have *more* time to devote to the things which interest you is certainly no reason for passing up the possibilities of the present hour.

Suppose, for instance, that by a readjustment of your rising-time, you now have an extra half-hour before you leave your home for your day's activities. What can you do with it?

The following list of possible ways to utilize that salvaged half-hour is entirely illustrative. It does not begin to cover *all* the ways in which it could be used. It probably includes some in which you would not be the least bit interested. But just to give you some ideas, here's the list:

(1) Spend more time on your daily newspaper. *Read* the editorials, or the items on the business page, or other features of the paper which appeal to you, instead of merely *skimming* over them or *skipping* them altogether.

(2) Read your business papers or professional magazines, current periodicals or books which may be of real practical value to you but which hitherto you just "haven't had the time" to read.

(3) Write some of those letters you have been putting off. Write *more* letters or notes than you have ever written before. You can make a lot of people happy by merely dropping them a line congratulating them on something they have recently achieved, or passing along an idea that might interest them.

(4) Devote the extra half-hour to your hobby, whatever it is. If you haven't a hobby, because you have always been too busy, start one.

(5) What about some of those household chores, those repair jobs, those furniture rearrangements, and those scores of other things to be done around the house which you have always been going to "get at" *some time* but never seem to

find the time or are too tired to take care of when you happen to think of them?

(6) You *could* use that extra half hour for something you probably need very much—exercise. If one form or another of indoor exercise does not appeal to you, a half-hour's walk every morning would probably mean more to you healthwise than anything else you are now doing to keep yourself in proper physical condition. If you could use this time to *walk* part of the way to your daily work instead of riding, you could get *double* value out of it: you would get the benefit of the exercise and, while you were walking, you could turn your mind to some constructive planning.

(7) How about extending your acquaintanceship with some of your local or neighborhood tradesmen? Some of them at least will be open early enough to make a friendly visit feasible. You may even find among your neighbors some who will be glad to follow your example and join you in your early morning walk.

(8) If you have youngsters in your family, could you not put that extra half-hour to profitable use by spending it with them? Have you always been able to give your youngsters all the time you would like to spend with them? Are there not some beneficial activities you could take up jointly with your family in the morning if you didn't always have to rush for that train? Even if you used some of that extra time to eat your breakfast more leisurely and to discuss things with your family calmly and unhurriedly instead of "on the run," would that not be a gain for everybody concerned?

(9) And if you have no youngsters of your own are there not some neighbor's kids you would like to know better and

who might like to know you? If you had a little more time in the morning, instead of always being late for work, could you not use some of it profitably getting to *know* some of the kids instead of merely hurrying past them as you do now?

(10) If your work is of a nature that you can do some of it at home, you could certainly put that early morning half-hour to no more effective use than by devoting it to some of that homework you brought home with you the night before. Remember that that salvaged half-hour is not only *extra* time but is probably the *best* half-hour you will have all day. Mentally and physically refreshed by your night's sleep, you are probably in better condition then to tackle anything than at any other time of the day.

But, you may ask, conceding that considerable can be done with an extra half-hour made available regularly every morning, what, if anything, can be done with shorter periods —the five minutes you have to wait for a train, or in the waiting-room of your dentist or doctor, or in the reception room of some business man you are calling on?

That is a fair question and presents an extremely important problem for those who believe in time-thrift. Probably nobody likes to be kept cooling his heels waiting for an interview, but such experiences are particularly irritating to those who are allergic to time-wasting. Furthermore, the short snatches of extra time which become available to those who make the effort to salvage them mount up to a respectable total in the course of a day.

If these odd moments are to be put to effective use, you must plan *in advance* to capture and use them.

One obvious way to prepare for such opportunities is to

provide yourself with reading matter which you can carry handily in a pocket. How many of us find time to read even a small fraction of the treasures which are available to us? *Some day,* of course, we are going to read all those great books which we have so far missed, but right now it is tough enough even to keep up with current literature. Of course, it would not be so tough if you carried around with you a pocket edition of one of those books you have promised yourself to read "some day," and started reading it *now*— whenever you have five or ten minutes that you cannot very well put to any other use. It may be the five minutes you feel you can spare in your own office because you spend less time at lunch than usual, or the five or ten minutes in your own home before or after meals or between other activities.

The fact that pocket-size editions of books and pamphlets are available on almost any subject provides one complete answer to those who say or think that you cannot do anything useful with the small fragments of time which time-thrift offers to all.

But if reading does not provide the answer to the problem in a particular case, other solutions are available to all. You can use some of those salvaged minutes for *relaxation* in whatever form the conditions may permit. At the very worst, you can always close your eyes and rest. Or you may work out a cross-word puzzle, if you have one handy. You can devote the time to some constructive *thinking* or *planning.* You can make notes in a pocket memo book of things to be done or remembered. You may be able to carry out one or more of the "things to be done" which your note-book brings to your attention. If a telephone is handy, you can make one of those calls you planned to make "some time." Or if writing facilities are at hand, you can get off one of those friendly notes you planned to write. You can always review the events of the day or of yesterday, and perhaps develop a new slant or course of action which had not occurred to you before. Or you can map out in your mind a plan of campaign or some other activity in which you are planning to engage.

In the great majority of cases, perhaps, you will reap the benefit of salvaged minutes automatically by getting at your next activity just that much sooner. Whether you are your own boss or are working for somebody else, the fact that you can put more time into what you are doing will usually pay off in one way or another. If you are sincerely time-conscious, the knowledge that you have *used* time instead of *wasting* it will be its own reward.

It is undoubtedly true that many people who have never given a moment's thought to the possibilities of time-thrift may nevertheless use their spare moments occasionally or frequently as suggested in this chapter. Even those who say they want nothing to do with time-thrift may show more respect for time than they are willing to admit. In other words, many people practice time-thrift without being aware of it or even while they are making fun of it. But these things only emphasize the fact that it is both desirable and *feasible* for those who *are* time-conscious to utilize the small scraps of time that become available as well as the longer stretches.

The key fact to remember in this connection is that *no* time need be wasted if you take the necessary but simple steps to use it.

No effort is made to list here the many ways in which leisure can be most profitably used. Hundreds of books have been published on that general subject. Anyone who is in-

terested in putting to more effective use the additional leisure which the practice of time-thrift will yield is advised to
read some of the many fine books on the subject which are
available at his library. Perhaps one of the most appropriate
ways to use some of that extra time you are going to make
for yourself would be in reading one or more of such works.

One book which is right on the beam is "How to Gain An
Extra Hour Every Day," by Ray Josephs (Dutton, New
York, 1955). Mr. Josephs devotes relatively little space
to the reasons for saving time, nor to the uses to which saved
time can be put. Perhaps he figures that those phases of the
subject are adequately covered in other books, such as this
one, which he quotes in another connection.

Instead the author assumes that his readers are already
time-conscious and, for one purpose or another, want to
salvage some of the time they are now losing. And so he
presents in the book's 192 pages no less than 243 specific
ways in which most of us could save time.

Most of the time-saving recipes in this book are based on
the actual habits of some of our best-known, busiest people.
Among them are such outstanding people of accomplish-
ment as Sir Winston Churchill, John Foster Dulles, President
Eisenhower, Henry Ford II, Arthur Godfrey, Dr. Norman
Vincent Peale, Dr. Daniel Poling, Mrs. Eleanor Roosevelt
and ex-president Harry S. Truman.

Not all the time-saving methods used by these and others,
as described in this book, could, of course, be put to use
by every individual. But the theory of the book is that anybody ought to be able to utilize at least enough of them to
give him an extra hour every day.

No matter what your present activity—or inactivity—

may be, here are hundreds of ways in which you can stop *wasting* time, which is, of course, the only way in which you can actually *gain* time.

Another recent book which has had wide circulation and which should be useful to almost anyone who wants to make the most of the time he gains through better time-management methods is "How to Live 365 Days a Year," by the late Dr. John A. Schindler (Prentice-Hall, New York, 1954).

In this book, Dr. Schindler, a Mid-Western medical man who was accidentally killed in 1957, undertook to prove that much of our unhappiness stems from just one basic cause which he calls "emotionally induced illness." He spells out dozens of ways by which such illness can be avoided or cured. The fact is, according to the doctor, that most of our troubles are of our own making, since by adopting more *positive attitudes* we can eliminate the factors responsible for them.

Everybody could benefit by following Dr. Schindler's simple, practical and logical blueprint for happiness.

One of the doctor's recommendations is based squarely on an appreciation of the value of time. If we want happiness, the only way we can find it, he points out, is by taking advantage of the *present*.

"The only moment we ever live is the present moment," he declares. "It is the only time *we ever have* to be happy." The best insurance for a satisfactory future, he advised, "is to handle the present hour properly, do a good job of living now, be effective in your work, your thinking, your pleasantness, your helpfulness to other people, RIGHT NOW. Yes, RIGHT NOW. The future will turn out to be as good as your present if you keep on handling THE PRESENT MOMENT correctly. That is an important trick."

Of course the doctor was right, and his book reveals how almost anyone who really wants to be happy can achieve his goal.

For those who are planning to retire or expect to be retired, the problem of how to employ one's time usefully and effectively when all your time is your own is naturally an important one. It looms even bigger for those who have been following time-management principles during their working lives and will therefore have more time available for new activities after retirement than the time-wasters to whom retirement will merely mean more time to waste!

Many books are available for those who want suggestions on how to make the best use of the extra time they will have after they retire. In April, 1956, the New York Public Library published an extensive list of those they recommended, with a brief description of each. Among those which sound as if they might be useful, I note the following:

Best Years of Your Life, by Marie B. Ray

Live Better After Fifty, by Ray Giles

Six Ways to Retire, by Paul W. Boynton

The Second Forty Years, by Edward J. Stieglitz

Money-Making Hobbies, by Joseph Leeming

Ways and Means to Successful Retirement, by Evelyn Colby and John G. Forrest

Jobs After Retirement, by Maxwell Lehman and Morton Yarmon

Every Woman's Guide to Spare-Time Income, by the same authors.

An excellent idea is offered by the Library for those who may want to put some of their salvaged time to constructive use in service to others.

"For the person whose life is no longer circumscribed by the demands of business or family," the Library suggests, "service in one of the many worthwhile organizations which depend, in part, on volunteers to carry on their work can be most rewarding." In New York, information about such opportunities can be obtained from the Welfare and Health Council which maintains a Central Volunteer Bureau, the Library points out. No doubt similar opportunities are available in other cities.

The main purpose of these pages is to reiterate the all-important fact that, as Gladstone said, "thrift of time will repay you in after life with a usury of profit beyond your most sanguine dreams."

To provide a daily reminder of the priceless value of time in the language of the wise men of all ages, a "Time-Thrift Calendar" is presented in the pages which follow. The 366 quotations selected—one for every day of the year, including Leap Year—were culled from thousands of similar epigrams and observations with which our literature abounds. They were chosen because, in the author's opinion, they provide the kind of inspiration and encouragement which even those who believe in time-thrift may find helpful.

CHAPTER VIII

A TIME-THRIFT CALENDAR

JANUARY 1

RESOLVED, to live with all my might while I do live.
RESOLVED, never to lose one moment of time, to improve it the most profitable way I possibly can.

—Jonathan Edwards

JANUARY 2

Thrift of time will repay you in after life with a usury of profit beyond your most sanguine dreams.

—William Ewart Gladstone

JANUARY 3

Every day is a vessel into which very much may be poured if one will really fill it up. *—Goethe*

JANUARY 4

Nothing lies on our hands with such uneasiness as time. Wretched and thoughtless creatures! In the only place where covetousness were a virtue, we turn prodigals. *—Addison*

JANUARY 5

Every man's life lies within the present; for the past is spent and done with, and the future is uncertain.

—Marcus Aurelius

JANUARY 6

The best of all ways to lengthen our days is to steal a few hours from the night.   *—Moore*

JANUARY 7

We are here to add what we can to, not to get what we can from, Life.   *—Sir William Osler*

JANUARY 8

There is no wealth but life.   *—Ruskin*

JANUARY 9

To what end would longer life serve you? If it is that you wish to improve your wisdom and virtue, have you employed the little time that you have? If not, why complain that more is not given you?   *—Dandemis*

JANUARY 10

He only is rich who owns the day. There is no king, rich man, fairy or demon who possesses such power as that.
    —Emerson

JANUARY 11

He liveth long who liveth well!
All else is being flung away;
He liveth longest who can tell
Of true things only done each day.
    —Horatius Bonar

JANUARY 12

Hold the fleet angel fast until he bless thee!
—Nathaniel Cotton

JANUARY 13

All my possessions for a moment of time!
—Last words of Queen Elizabeth, I

JANUARY 14

The passing moment is an edifice which the Omnipotent cannot rebuild.   *—Emerson*

JANUARY 15

We all of us complain of the shortness of time and yet have much more than we know what to do with.

We are always complaining that our days are few, and acting as though there would be no end of them.   *—Seneca*

JANUARY 16

The wise count the hours.
—Sundial owned by the WISE *family*

JANUARY 17

Our grand business in life is not to see what lies dimly in the distance, but to do what lies already at hand.
—Thomas Carlyle

JANUARY 18

He who postpones the hour of living as he ought is like the rustic who waits for the river to pass along before he crosses; but it glides on and will glide on forever.   *—Horace*

JANUARY 19

No great thing is created suddenly, any more than a bunch of grapes or a fig. If you tell me that you desire a fig, I answer you that there must be time. Let it first blossom, then bear fruit, then ripen.   *—Epictetus*

JANUARY 20

Oh, trifle not with life—'tis but an hour;
Redeem it every moment, day by day.
  —Horatius Bonar

JANUARY 21

Time was, is past: thou canst not it recall;
Time is, thou hast: employ the portion small;
Time future, is not, and may never be:
Time present is the only time for thee.
  —Anonymous

JANUARY 22

Tomorrow—oh, 'twill never be
If we should live a thousand years!
Our time is all today, today,
The same though changed; and while it flies
With still small voice the moments say:
Today, today, be wise, be wise.
  —James Montgomery

JANUARY 23

Tomorrow comes and we are where? Then let us live today.   *—Schiller*

JANUARY 24

And if I drink oblivion of a day
So shorten I the stature of my soul.
                              —*George Meredith*

JANUARY 25

Every moment may be put to some use and that with
more pleasure than if unemployed.   —*Lord Chesterfield*

JANUARY 26

Like coral insects multitudinous
The minutes are where our life is made.
                              —*Jean Ingelow*

JANUARY 27

The reason I beat the Austrians is that they did not know
the value of five minutes.   —*Napoleon*

JANUARY 28

Pastime is a word which should never be used but in a
bad sense; it is vile to say a thing is agreeable because it
helps to pass the time away.   —*William Shenstone*

JANUARY 29

Youth is not rich in Time, it may be poor;
Part with it as with Money, sparing; pay
No moment but in purchase of its worth;
And what it's worth, ask Death-beds; they can tell
                              —*Young*

January 30

Do not defer to the evening what this morning may accomplish. Idleness is the parent of want and pain; but the labor of virtue brings happiness.   *—Dandemis*

January 31

I have hardly words for the estimate I form of the sluggard, male or female, that has formed the habit of wasting the early prime of day in bed.   *—Flint*

February 1

A day is a more magnificent cloth than any muslin; the mechanism that makes it is infinitely cunninger, and you shall not conceal the sleazy, fraudulent, rotten hours you have slipped into the piece; nor fear that any honest thread, or straighter steel, or more inflexible shaft, will not testify in the web.   *—Emerson*

February 2

We sleep, but the loom of life never stops, and the pattern which was weaving when the sun went down is weaving when it comes up in the morning.   *—Henry Ward Beecher*

February 3

It is better to be doing the most insignificant thing than to reckon even half-an-hour insignificant.   *—Goethe*

February 4

The most useless day of all is that in which we have not laughed.   *—Chamfort*

FEBRUARY 5

Life is too short to waste
In critic peep or cynic bark,
Quarrel or reprimand:
'Twill soon be dark;
Up! Mind thine own aim, and
God speed the mark!

—Emerson

FEBRUARY 6

Not only is he idle who does nothing, but he that might be better employed. *—Socrates*

FEBRUARY 7

Be not as one who has ten thousand years to live.

—Marcus Aurelius

FEBRUARY 8

It matters not how long we live, but how.

—Philip J. Bailey

FEBRUARY 9

If you do your fair day's work, you are certain to get your fair day's wages—in praise or pudding, whichever happens to suit your taste. *—Alexander Smith*

FEBRUARY 10

Be wise today; 'tis madness to defer. *—Young*

FEBRUARY 11

To him who rises early in the morning, God gives help and lends His hand. *—Old French Proverb*

FEBRUARY 12

Tomorrow's hours may be less fortunate.

—Sundial Inscription

FEBRUARY 13

Oh, seize the instant time; you never will
With waters once passed impel the mill.

—Trench

FEBRUARY 14

Have you somewhat to do Tomorrow, do it Today.

—Benjamin Franklin

FEBRUARY 15

The soul of the sluggard desireth and hath nothing, but the
soul of the diligent shall be made fat.   *—Proverbs XIII:4*

FEBRUARY 16

There is not too much time for well doing, since the hour
passes away quickly.   *—Sundial Inscription*

FEBRUARY 17

Let not your recreations be lavish spenders of your time.

—Jeremy Taylor

FEBRUARY 18

Bind together your spare hours by the cord of some definite purpose and you know not how much you may accomplish. Gather up the fragments of your time that nothing
be lost.   *—William M. Taylor*

FEBRUARY 19

The greatest consideration which ought to influence the use of the present moment is the effect it must have on the time to come.   —*Samuel Johnson*

FEBRUARY 20

Very late in life when he was studying geometry, some one said to Lacydes, "Is it then a time for you to be learning now?" "If it is not," he replied, "when will it be?"

—*Diogenes Laertius*

FEBRUARY 21

While strength and years permit, endure labor.   —*Ovid*

FEBRUARY 22

If all the year were playing holidays
To sport would be as tedious as to work.

—*Shakespeare:* King Henry IV

FEBRUARY 23

The present only is thine own.   —*Sundial Inscription*

FEBRUARY 24

My days are swifter than a weaver's shuttle. —*Job VII:6*

FEBRUARY 25

He that hopes to look back hereafter with satisfaction upon past years, must learn to know the value of single minutes, and endeavor to let no particle of time fall useless to the ground.   —*Samuel Johnson*

FEBRUARY 26

To someone complaining that he had not enough time, a poor Indian chief made a wiser reply than any philosopher: "I suppose you have all there is."

—*Emerson:* Works and Days

FEBRUARY 27

It would be thought a hard government that should tax its people one-tenth part of their time, to be employed in its service; but idleness taxes many of us much more.

—*Benjamin Franklin*

FEBRUARY 28

I shall ever regret the time which, while young, I lost in mere idleness, and in doing nothing. The value of moments, when cast up, is immense if well employed; if thrown away, their loss is irrecoverable.   —*Lord Chesterfield*

FEBRUARY 29

Count that day lost whose low descending sun
Views from thy hand no worthy action done.

—*Anonymous*

MARCH 1

Knowest thou the meaning of this day? What thou canst do today wisely attempt to do.   —*Carlyle*

MARCH 2

For my own private satisfaction, I had rather be master of my own time than own a diadem.   —*Bishop Berkeley*

MARCH 3

For the hair's breadth of time assigned to thee, live rationally.   —*Marcus Aurelius*

MARCH 4

This instant is yours; the next belongs still to futurity, and you do not know what it may bring forth.   —*Dandemis*

MARCH 5

Dost thou love life? Then waste not time, for that is the stuff life is made of.   —*Benjamin Franklin*

MARCH 6

It is my firm conviction that man has only himself to blame if his life appears to him at any time void of interest and pleasure. Man may make life what he pleases, and give it as much worth, both for himself and others, as he has energy for.   —*Humboldt*

MARCH 7

A well spent day brings happy sleep.

—*Leonardo da Vinci*

MARCH 8

What a solemn and striking admonition to youth is that inscribed on the dial at All Souls, Oxford—*periunt et imputantur*—the hours perish and are laid to our charge; for time like life, can never be recalled.   —*Samuel Smiles*

MARCH 9

Sloth has frequently and justly been denominated the rust of the soul.   —*Rev. John Todd*

MARCH 10

You wake up in the morning, and lo! your purse is magically filled with twenty-four hours of the unmanufactured tissue of the universe of your life! It is yours! It is the most precious of possessions.   —*Arnold Bennett*

MARCH 11

It is one of the illusions that the present hour is not the critical, decisive hour.   —*Emerson*

MARCH 12

He who would do some great things in this short life must apply himself to the work with such concentration of his forces as to idle spectators, who live only to amuse themselves, looks like insanity.   —*John Foster*

MARCH 13

We always have time enough if we will but use it aright.
                    —*Goethe*

MARCH 14

The real secret of how to use time is to pack it as you would a portmanteau, filling up the small places with small things.   —*Sir Henry Haddow*

MARCH 15

Thou knowest my hour—not thine!

—Sundial Inscription

MARCH 16

Let your sleep be necessary and healthful, not idle and expensive of time, beyond the needs and conveniences of nature. *—Jeremy Taylor*

MARCH 17

When Time who steals our years away
Shall steal our pleasures too,
The memory of the past will stay
And half our joys renew;
Then talk no more of future gloom
Our joys shall always last,
For hope shall brighten days to come
And memory gild the past.

—Thomas Moore

MARCH 18

The time of life is short; to spend that shortness basely, 'twere too long. *—Shakespeare*

MARCH 19

Of all work that produces results, nine-tenths must be drudgery. *—Bishop of Exeter*

MARCH 20

In a thousand years we shall all forget
The things that trouble us now.

—Adam Lindsay Gordon

MARCH 21

Don't waste life in doubts and fears; spend yourself on the work before you, well assured that the right performance of this hour's duties will be the best preparation for the hours or ages which follow it.   —*Emerson*

MARCH 22

Laziness grows in people; it begins in cobwebs and ends in iron chains. The more business a man has to do the more he is able to accomplish, for he learns to economize his time.   —*Sir Matthew Hale*

MARCH 23

Gently but swiftly flows on the hour that can never return
Consider well that thou lose not the day without its work
                    —*Sundial Inscription*

MARCH 24

The more we sleep the less we live.   —*Old Maxim*

MARCH 25

Time is the present hour, the past is fled;
Live! live today! tomorrow never yet
On any human being rose or set.
                    —*Marsden*

MARCH 26

Each day is a branch of the tree of life, laden heavily with fruit. If we lie down lazily beneath it, we may starve; but if we shake the branches, some of the fruit may fall on us.
                    —*Longfellow*

MARCH 27

Catch then, Oh catch the transient hour
Improve each moment as it flies.

—*Samuel Johnson*

MARCH 28

Like fishes let the hours be caught.

—*Sundial Inscription*

MARCH 29

Tomorrow is that lamp upon the marsh, which a traveller
   never reacheth;
Reconcile conviction with delay, and Tomorrow is a fatal lie:
Frighten resolutions into action, Tomorrow is a wholesome
   truth.

—*Tupper*

MARCH 30

All that time is lost which might be better employed.

—*Rousseau*

MARCH 31

Make use of time if thou lovest eternity; yesterday cannot
be recalled; tomorrow cannot be assured; only today is
thine, which if thou procrastinate thou loseth; and which
lost is lost forever. One day is worth two tomorrows.

—*Quarles*

APRIL 1

He that gathereth in summer is a wise son, but he that
sleepeth in harvest is a son that causeth shame.

—*Proverbs X:5*

APRIL 2

Is not life a hundred times too short for us to bore ourselves?   —*Nietzsche*

APRIL 3

At sunrise every soul is born again.   —*Walter Malone*

APRIL 4

Time stays long enough for those who use it.
                                        —*Leonardo da Vinci*

APRIL 5

Dally not with time, the wise man's treasure though fools are lavish with it.   —*Anonymous*

APRIL 6

Whatsoever thy hand findeth to do do it with thy whole might. Work while it is called Today, for the Night cometh wherein no man can work.   —*Carlyle*

APRIL 7

The sum of wisdom is that the time is never lost that is devoted to work.   —*Emerson*

APRIL 8

Employ the time well if thou meanest to gain leisure, and since thou art not sure of a minute, throw not away an hour.
                                            —*Franklin*

April 9

The wise prove and the foolish confess by their conduct, that a life of employment is the only life worth leading.

—Goethe

April 10

Life being very short, and the quiet hours of it few, we ought to waste none of them reading valueless books.

—Ruskin

April 11

In delay we waste our lights in vain; like lamps by day.

—Shakespeare

April 12

You neglect duties, public and private, and satisfy conscience that you have not time to fulfill them all. But the wasted hours cry out against you.   *—Rev. John Todd*

April 13

He that from childhood has made rising betimes familiar to him will not waste the best part of his life in drowsiness and lying abed.   *—Locke*

April 14

So here hath been dawning
Another blue day:
Think! wilt thou let it
Slip useless away?

—Carlyle

April 15

Oh! how many deeds
Of deathless virtue, and immortal crime,
The world had wanted, had the actor said
I will do this tomorrow!

—Lord John Russell

April 16

Who is he who does not always find himself doing something less than his best task? "What are you doing?" "Oh, nothing; I have been doing thus, or I shall be doing so and so, but now I am only—" Ah! poor dupe, will you never slip out of the web of the master juggler?   *—Emerson*

April 17

Gather roses while they bloom
Tomorrow is yet far away
Moments lost have no room
In tomorrow or today

—Gleim

April 18

Lives of great men all remind us
We can make our lives sublime
And departing, leave behind us
Footprints on the sands of time.

—Longfellow

APRIL 19

Tomorrow I will live, the fool does say: today itself's too late; the wise lived yesterday.   —*Martial*

APRIL 20

Time wasted is existence; used, is life.   —*Young*

APRIL 21

Multitude of hours pilfered away by what the bard who sang of the Enchanter Indolence hath called "good natured lounging," and behold a map of my collegiate life.

—*Wordsworth*

APRIL 22

The man who goes alone can start today; but he who travels with another must wait until that other is ready.

—*Thoreau*

APRIL 23

Our time is a very shadow that passeth away.

—*Solomon II:5*

APRIL 24

If time be heavy on your hands
Are there no beggars at your gates,
Nor any poor about your lands?
Oh! teach the orphan boy to read
Or teach the orphan girl to sew.

—*Tennyson*

APRIL 25

Why work I not? The veriest mite that sports its one-day life within the sunny beam has its stern duties.

—*Alexander Smith*

APRIL 26

Leisure is time for doing something useful; this leisure the diligent man will obtain, but the lazy man never.

—*Benjamin Franklin*

APRIL 27

There is so much to be done that we ought to begin quickly to bestir ourselves.

—*Emerson*

APRIL 28

The gay who would be counted wise
Think all delight in pastime lies
Nor heed they what the wise condemn;
Whilst they pass time—time passes them!

—*Sundial Inscription*

APRIL 29

I would have inscribed on the curtains of your bed and the walls of your chamber: "If you do not rise early, you can never make progress in anything." If you do not set apart your hours of reading, if you suffer yourself or anyone else to break in upon them, your days will slip through your hands unprofitable and frivolous, and really unenjoyed by yourself."

—*Lord Chatham*

April 30

When the mason carries up the wall, the course of the brick which he laid yesterday is the foundation on which he is laying another course today; and all that you do today on the structure which you are building, will remain as the basis for that which you do tomorrow.

—Henry Ward Beecher

May 1

Like our shadows our wishes lengthen as our sun declines.

—Young

May 2

I knock unbidden once at every gate
If sleeping, wake; if feasting, rise before
I turn away. It is the hour of fate.

—John J. Ingalls

May 3

Fill the unforgiving minute
With sixty seconds' worth of distance run.

—Kipling

May 4

No change, great or marked, in your general course, is necessary to make new and rich acquisitions; only save every moment of time which you now throw away, and you will be able to do anything.   *—Rev. John Todd*

May 5

Hold fast by the present. Every situation—nay, every moment—is of infinite worth, for it is the representative of a whole eternity.   *—Goethe*

May 6

I wasted time and now doth time waste me.

—Shakespeare: Richard II

May 7

Striking from the Calendar
Unborn Tomorrow and dead Yesterday.

—Fitzgerald: Omar Khayyám

May 8

Time was, Time is, but Time shall be no more.

—Marsden

May 9

Life, however short, is made shorter by waste of time.

—Samuel Johnson

May 10

Much may be done in those little shreds and patches of time which every day produces and which most men throw away, but which nevertheless will make at the end of it no small deduction from the life of man.   *—Colton*

May 11

What is man if his chief good and market of his time be but to sleep and feed?   *—Shakespeare:* Hamlet

May 12

Shun delays, they breed remorse; take thy time while time is lent thee.   —*Southwell*

May 13

Miss not the occasion; by the forelock take that subtle power, the never-halting time.   —*Wordsworth*

May 14

Nothing is more precious than time and those who misspend it are the greatest of all prodigals.   —*Theophrastus*

May 15

No man has learned anything rightly until he knows that every day is Doomsday.   —*Emerson*

May 16

How much time he gains who does not look to see what his neighbor says or does or thinks, but only at what he does himself, to make it just and holy.   —*Marcus Aurelius*

May 17

Never returning, hours glide away
Thou, though much yearning, canst not delay;
Laboring, learning, spend thou the day,
Indolence spurning, watch thou and pray.
                              —*Sundial Inscription*

May 18

As if thou could kill time without injuring Eternity!
                              —*Thoreau*

MAY 19

They who await no gifts from Chance have conquered Fate.
                                                    —*Matthew Arnold*

MAY 20

I fly away even whilst thou watchest me.
                                        —*Sundial Inscription*

MAY 21

Make use of time, let not advantage slip,
Fair flowers that are not gathered in their prime
Rot and consume themselves in little time.
                        —*Shakespeare:* Venus and Adonis

MAY 22

One life—a little gleam of time between two eternities.
                                                    —*Carlyle*

MAY 23

Days that are past are gone forever, and those that are to come may not come to you; therefore, employ the present without regretting the loss of what is past or depending too much upon what is not yet here.   —*Dandemis*

MAY 24

There is no remedy for time misspent;
No healing for the waste of idleness,
Whose very languor is a punishment
Heavier than active souls can fear or guess.
                                        —*Sir Aubrey De Vere*

May 25

Time is like a ship which never anchors: while I am on board I had better do those things that may profit me at landing. —*Owen Feltham*

May 26

We would accomplish many more things if we did not think of them as impossible.   —*Chrétien Malesherbes*

May 27

That part of our time which we can spend wholly at our own choice is very small. Of the few moments which are left in our disposal we should be so frugal as to let none of them slip from us without some equivalent.

—*Samuel Johnson*

May 28

That time which is good enough for nothing else we dedicate to virtue, and only propose to live at an age that very few people attain.   —*Seneca*

May 29

He lives twice who can once employ
The present well, and ev'n the past enjoy.

—*Pope*

May 30

Do not shorten the morning by getting up late; look upon it as the quintessence of life, as to a certain extent sacred.

—*Schopenhauer*

May 31

The utility of living does not consist in the length of days, but in the well husbanding and improving of time.

—Montaigne

June 1

Thank God every morning when you get up that you have something to do that day which must be done, whether you like it or not. Being forced to work, and forced to do your best, will breed in you temperance and self-control, diligence and strength of will, cheerfulness and content, and a hundred virtues which the idle can never know.

—Charles Kingsley

June 2

Future or Past, no richer secret folds
O friendless Present, than thy bosom holds.

—Emerson

June 3

There is no moment like the present. The man who will not execute his resolutions when they are fresh upon him can have no hope from them afterwards.

—Maria Edgeworth

June 4

Today is ours; what do we fear?
Today is ours; we have it here.
Let's treat it kindly, that it may
Wish, at least, with us to stay.

—Cowley

JUNE 5

Redeem mine hours—the space is brief—
While in my glass the sand grains shiver,
And measureless thy joy and grief
When Time and thou shall part forever.

—Sir Walter Scott

JUNE 6

Each day is rich in potentialities. We can either use the passing hours to implement our plans, realize our dreams, strengthen our foundations, or we may treat these hours with unthinking indifference, the moments slipping through our fingers like fine sand on the shore.   *—"Callisthenes"*

JUNE 7

Now, or when?   *—Sundial Inscription*

JUNE 8

Yet a little sleep, a little slumber, a little folding of the hands to rest; so shall thy poverty come like a robber and thy want as an armed man.   *—Proverbs VI:10*

JUNE 9

Each is given a bag of tools,
A shapeless mass,
A book of rules;
And each must make
Ere life is flown
A stumbling block
Or a stepping stone.

—R. L. Sharpe

JUNE 10

The certainty that life cannot be long and the probability that it will be shorter than nature allows, ought to waken every man to the active prosecution of whatever he is desirous to perform.   —*Samuel Johnson*

JUNE 11

Gather ye rosebuds while ye may
Old Time is still a-flying
And this same flower which smiles today
Tomorrow will be dying.

—*Robert Herrick*

JUNE 12

The same object seen from three different points of view —the past, the present and the future—often exhibits three different faces to us; like those signboards over shop doors which represent the face of a lion as we approach, of a man when we are in front, and of an ass when we have passed.

—*Longfellow*

JUNE 13

Trust no future, howe'er pleasant!
Let the dead Past bury its dead!
Act, act in the Living Present!
Heart within, and God o'erhead!

—*Longfellow*

JUNE 14

Heavens! Can you then waste, in shameful wise,
Your few important days of trial here?

—*Thomson*

JUNE 15

Give me the calendar as my guide, says the man of wisdom. I am interested in knowing how much time I have in which to do the things I want to do.   —*Morris-Jones*

JUNE 16

What a folly to dread the thought of throwing life away at once, and yet have no regard to throwing it away by parcels and piecemeal.   —*John Howe*

JUNE 17

The use of history is to give value to the present hour and its duty.   —*Emerson*

JUNE 18

To fritter away the hours is saddening, when our working hours are so tragically few. Yet there are men who squander the treasure as if the supply were unending and mortal span had no limit at all.   —*"Callisthenes"*

JUNE 19

To choose time is to save time; and an unseasonable motion is but beating the air.   —*Bacon*

JUNE 20

Sloth views the towers of Fame with envious eyes
Desirous but still impotent to rise.

—*Shenstone*

June 21

The whole life of man is but a point of time; let us enjoy it therefore while it lasts, and not spend it to no purpose.

—*Plutarch*

June 22

Reverence for the deeds of our ancestors is a treacherous sentiment. Their merit was not to reverence the old, but to honor the present moment; and we falsely make them excuses for the very habit which they hated and defied.

—*Emerson*

June 23

Man cannot call the brimming instant back,
Time's an affair of instants spun to days,
If man must make an instant gold or black,
Let him, he may, but Time must go his ways.

—*Masefield*

June 24

There can be no persevering industry without a deep sense of the value of time.   —*Mrs. Lydia H. Sigourney*

June 25

Nae man can tether time or tide.   —*Robert Burns*

June 26

Man is like a thing of naught; his time passeth away like a shadow.   —*Psalms CXLIV:4*

JUNE 27

Let us live as men who are sometime to grow old and to whom it will be the most dreadful of all evils to count their past years by their follies.   —*Samuel Johnson*

JUNE 28

All my past life is mine no more;
    The flying hours are gone;
The time that is to come is not;
    How can it then be mine?
The present moment's all my lot.

—*Earl of Rochester*

JUNE 29

You may waste but cannot stop me.

—*Sundial Inscription*

JUNE 30

How profitable it is for everyone of us to be reminded, as we are reminded when we make ourselves aware of the derivation of diligence from "diligo," to love, that the only secret of true industry in our work is love of that work!

—*Trench*

JULY 1

Tomorrow, tomorrow, not today,
Hear the lazy people say.

—*Weisse*

July 2

Tomorrow, didst thou say? Go to—I will not hear of it. Tomorrow! 'tis a sharper who stakes his penury against thy plenty—who takes thy ready cash and pays thee naught but wishes, hopes and promises, the currency of idots. Tomorrow! it is a period nowhere to be found in all the hoary registers of time, unless perchance in the fool's calendar. Wisdom disclaims the word. 'Tis fancy's child and folly is its father; wrought of such stuff as dreams are and baseless as the fantastic visions of the evening.   —*Nathaniel Cotton*

July 3

You will never "find" time for anything. If you want time you must make it.   —*Charles Buxton*

July 4

My rule always was to do the business of the day in the day.   —*Duke of Wellington*

July 5

Whoever has tasted the breath of morning, knows that the most invigorating and delightful hours of the day are commonly spent in bed; though it is the evident intention of nature that we should enjoy and profit by them.

—*Southey*

July 6

Love not sleep lest thou come to poverty.

—*Proverbs XX:13*

JULY 7

Alas! it is not till time with reckless hand has torn out half the leaves from the Book of Human Life to light the fires of passion from day to day that man begins to see that the leaves which remain are few in number.   —*Longfellow*

JULY 8

Time is what we want most, but what, alas! we use worst.
—*Penn*

JULY 9

A man's time, when well husbanded, is like a cultivated field, of which a few acres produce more of what is useful to life than extensive provinces, even of the richest soil, when overrun with weeds and brambles.   —*Hume*

JULY 10

Defer not till tomorrow to be wise
Tomorrow's sun to thee may never rise.
—*William Congreve*

JULY 11

The sluggard is wiser in his own conceit than seven men who can render a reason.   —*Proverbs XXVI:16*

JULY 12

As we lose the present hour by delaying from day to day to execute what we ought to do immediately, so most of us take occasion to sit still and throw away the time in our possession by retrospect on what is past.
—*Sir Robert Steele*

July 13

If men were weaned from their sauntering humor wherein they let a good part of their lives run uselessly away, they would acquire skill in hundreds of things.   —*Locke*

July 14

Oh! that thou would use the hour which will not return.
—*Sundial Inscription*

July 15

It was a favorite expression of Theophrastus that time was the most valuable thing a man could spend.
—*Diogenes Laertius*

July 16

Lost, yesterday, somewhere between sunrise and sunset, two golden hours, each set with sixty diamond minutes. No reward is offered, for they are gone forever.
—*Horace Mann*

July 17

The time to be happy is now,
The place to be happy is here,
The way to be happy is to make others so.
—*Robert G. Ingersoll*

July 18

So teach us to number our days that we may apply our hearts unto wisdom.   —*Psalms XC:12*

July 19

It is later than you think.   —*Sundial Inscription*

July 20

The past is gone. Let the dead past bury it. But he is richer than the angels who has left what you have left.

—*James Baldwin Brown*

July 21

Regret for time wasted may become a power for good in the time that remains. And the time that remains is time enough, if we will only stop the waste, and the idle, useless regretting.   —*Arthur Brisbane*

July 22

It is not so much the hours that tell, as the way we use them. Life must be measured rather by depth than by length; by thought and action rather than by time.

—*Lord Avebury*

July 23

The days come and go like muffled and veiled figures, sent from a distant friendly party; but they say nothing, and if we do not use the gifts they bring, they carry them as silently away.   —*Emerson*

July 24

Life, like every other blessing, derives its value from its use alone.   —*Samuel Johnson*

JULY 25

Every tomorrow has two handles. We can take hold of it with the handle of anxiety or the handle of faith. We should live for the future, and yet should find our life in the fidelities of the present; the last is only the method of the first.   —*Henry Ward Beecher*

JULY 26

The chief secret of comfort lies in not suffering trifles to vex one; and in prudently cultivating an undergrowth of small pleasures, since very great ones, alas! are let on long leases.   —*James Sharp*

JULY 27

Perhaps the most valuable result of all education is the ability to make yourself do the thing you have to do, when it ought to be done, whether you like it or not.
                                                                —*Thomas Henry Huxley*

JULY 28

The golden moments in the stream of life rush past us, and we see nothing but sand; the angels come to visit us, and we only know them when they are gone.   —*George Eliot*

JULY 29

Do not delay, do not delay,
The golden moments fly!
                                                                —*Longfellow*

July 30

My hours are made of sun and shade
Take heed of what thy hours are made
—*Sundial Inscription*

July 31

No man can promise himself even fifty years of life, but any man may, if he please, live in the proportion of fifty years in forty: let him rise early, that he may have the day before him. —*Colton*

August 1

Man does not live in the present, but with reverted eyes laments the past, or, heedless of the riches that surround him, stands on tiptoe to foresee the future. He cannot be happy and strong until he lives with nature in the present, above time. —*Emerson*

August 2

I recommend you take care of the minutes, for the hours will take care of themselves. —*Lord Chesterfield*

August 3

We must use every day and be done with it. You have done what you could. Some blunders and absurdities have crept in; forget them as soon as you can. Tomorrow is a new day; begin it well and serenely and with too high a spirit to be cumbered with your old nonsense. This day is all that is good and fair. It is too dear, with its hopes and invitations, to waste a moment on yesterdays. —*Emerson*

August 4

They do me wrong who say I come no more
When once I knock and fail to find you in;
For every day I stand outside your door,
And bid you wake, and rise to fight and win.

—*Walter Malone*

August 5

Let each man pass his days in that wherein his skill is greatest.   —*Propertius*

August 6

Early rising not only gives us more life in the same number of years, but adds, likewise, to their number.

—*Colton*

August 7

Be avaricious of time; do not give any amount without receiving it in value; only allow the hours to go from you with as much regret as you give to your gold; do not allow a single day to pass without increasing the treasure of your knowledge and virtue.   —*Letourneux*

August 8

I never knew a man come to greatness or eminence who lay abed late in the morning.   —*Swift*

August 9

Go to the ant, thou sluggard; consider her ways and be wise.   —*Proverbs VI:6*

AUGUST 10

It takes a long time to bring excellence to maturity.

—Publius Syrius

AUGUST 11

Nine men out of ten would have better health and more fun out of life if they spent less time in bed.

—Arnold Bennett

AUGUST 12

Chaucer, at Woodstock with the nightingales,
At sixty, wrote the Canterbury Tales;
Goethe, at Weimar, toiling to the last
Completed Faust when eighty years were past.

—Longfellow

AUGUST 13

As it would be great folly to shoe horses (as Nero did) with gold, so it is to spend time in trifles.   *—Mason*

AUGUST 14

Rise! for the day is passing
And you lie dreaming on;
The others have buckled their armor,
And forth to the fight are gone;
A place in the ranks awaits you
Each man has some part to play:
The Past and the Future are nothing
In the face of the stern Today.

—Adelaide Anne Procter

August 15

There is a past which is gone forever but there is a
future which is still our own.   —*F. W. Robertson*

August 16

The present is big with the future.   —*Leibnitz*

August 17

Seize now and here the hour that is, nor trust some later
day.   —*Horace*

August 18

Find time still to be learning something good and give
up being desultory.   —*Marcus Aurelius*

August 19

Eternity gives nothing back of what one leaves out of the
minutes.   —*Schiller*

August 20

The bell strikes one. We take no note of time but from
its loss.   —*Young*

August 21

Yesterday is but a dream
And tomorrow is only a vision
But today well lived makes every
Yesterday a dream of happiness and every
Tomorrow a vision of hope.

—*From the Sanskrit*

AUGUST 22

The King in a carriage may ride
And the Beggar may crawl at his side
But in the general race
They are travelling all at the same pace.

—Edward Fitzgerald

AUGUST 23

What next morn's sun may bring, forbear to ask,
But count each day that comes by gift of chance
So much to the good.

—Horace

AUGUST 24

Turn from blotted archives of the past
And find the future's pages white as snow.

—Walter Malone

AUGUST 25

Opportunities do not come with their value stamped on them. A day dawns quite like other days, but in that day a life faces us. To face every opportunity of life thoughtfully and ask its meaning bravely is the only way to meet supreme opportunities when they come.   *—Maltbie Babcock*

AUGUST 26

We shall do so much in the years to come
But what have we done today?
We shall give our gold in a princely sum,
But what did we give today?

—Nixon Waterman

August 27

O bright presence of Today, let me wrestle with thee gracious angel; I will not let thee go except thou bless me; bless me then, Today. —*M. F. Tupper*

August 28

Do today's work today. —*Sundial Inscription*

August 29

Remember how short my time is.

—*Psalms LXXXIX:47*

August 30

Bear today whate'er today may bring
'Tis the one way to make tomorrow sing.

—*Richard Le Gallienne*

August 31

I expect to pass through this world but once. Any good therefore that I can do, or any kindness that I can show to any fellow creature, let me do it NOW. Let me not defer nor neglect it, for I shall not pass this way again.

—*Stephen Degrellet*

September 1

The way to wealth is as plain as the way to market. It depends chiefly on two words—Industry and Frugality. That means waste neither Time nor Money, but make the best use of both. —*Benjamin Franklin*

SEPTEMBER 2

Lose this day loitering: 'Twill be the same story tomorrow —and the next more dilatory. Thus indecision brings its own delays, and days are lost lamenting over days. Are you in earnest? Seize this very minute—what you can do, or dream you can, begin it. Courage has genius, power and magic in it. Only engage and then the mind grows heated. Begin it and the work will be completed.   *—Goethe*

SEPTEMBER 3

What a man accomplishes depends mainly on what he does when he has nothing to do.   *—Buster Rothman*

SEPTEMBER 4

Use well the present moments as they fleet
Your life, however short, will be complete
If at its fatal ending you can say
I've lived and made the most of every day.
    —Sundial Inscription

SEPTEMBER 5

So the little moments, humble as they be,
Make the mighty ages of eternity.
    —Julia Fletcher Carney

SEPTEMBER 6

Every day is a little life; and our whole life is but a day repeated. Those, therefore, that dare lose a day, are dangerously prodigal; those that dare misspend it, desperate.
    —Joseph Hall

SEPTEMBER 7

Art is long, and Time is fleeting
And our hearts, though stout and brave
Still, like muffled drums, are beating
Funeral marches to the grave.

—Longfellow

SEPTEMBER 8

The time to come is no more ours than the past.

—Sundial Inscription

SEPTEMBER 9

The lives of most men are misspent for want of a certain end of their actions; wherein they do, as unwise archers, shoot away their arrows they know not at what mark.

—Joseph Hall

SEPTEMBER 10

Don't tell me what you will do
When you have time to spare;
Tell me what you did today
To ease a load of care.

—Grenville Kleiser

SEPTEMBER 11

Those who would bring great things to pass must rise early.   *—M. Henry*

SEPTEMBER 12

Procrastination is the thief of time.   *—Young*

SEPTEMBER 13

Time is painted with a forelock before, and bald behind, signifying thereby that we must take time by the forelock for when it is once passed there is no recalling it. —*Swift*

SEPTEMBER 14

Look not mournfully at the past—it comes not back again; wisely improve the present—it is thine.

—*Longfellow*

SEPTEMBER 15

He lives longest who is awake most hours.

—*German Proverb*

SEPTEMBER 16

As we use the hours so will the hours use us.

—*Sundial Inscription*

SEPTEMBER 17

He that hath time and looketh for a better time loseth time. —*Dr. Thomas Fuller*

SEPTEMBER 18

An Italian philosopher said that time was his estate; an estate, indeed, that will produce nothing without cultivation, but will always abundantly repay the labors of industry, and satisfy the most extensive desires, if no part of it be suffered to lie in waste by negligence, to be overrun by noxious plants or laid out for show rather than for use.

—*Samuel Johnson*

September 19

The greatest loss of time is delay and expectation, which depend upon the future. We let go the present, which we have in our power, and look forward to that which depends upon chance—and so quit a certainty for an uncertainty.

—*Seneca*

September 20

If time be of all things the most precious, wasting time must be the greatest prodigality, since lost time is never found again, and what we call time enough always proves little enough. Let us then be up and doing, and doing to purpose; so by diligence shall we do more with less perplexity.

—*Benjamin Franklin*

September 21

The hand of the diligent maketh rich. —*Proverbs X:4*

September 22

It is an undoubted truth that the less one has to do the less time one finds to do it in. Those who have a great deal of business, must buckle to it; and then they always find time enough to do it in. —*Lord Chesterfield*

September 23

It is within the reach of every man to live nobly, but within no man's power to live long. —*Seneca*

September 24

Wishing of all employments is the worst. —*Young*

SEPTEMBER 25

The reflections on a day well spent furnish us with joys more pleasing than ten thousand triumphs.

—Thomas a Kempis

SEPTEMBER 26

Too late hours in bed present an index to character. There is no mark so clear of a tendency to self-indulgence.

—Flint

SEPTEMBER 27

Indolence is the sleep of the mind.   *—Vauvenargues*

SEPTEMBER 28

Let us not suffer this precious lamp of life to burn in vain, or weeks, or days, or hours to slide away unemployed and useless.   *—Watts*

SEPTEMBER 29

Life is amply long for him who orders it properly.

—Seneca

SEPTEMBER 30

One thing is certain: that life flies.

—Edward Fitzgerald

OCTOBER 1

Time that is past thou never canst recall; of time to come thou art not sure at all; the present only is within thy power, so therefore now improve thy present hour.   *—Byron*

OCTOBER 2

Remember that time is money.   *—Benjamin Franklin*

OCTOBER 3

If you have but an hour, will you improve that hour, instead of idling it away?   *—Lord Chesterfield*

OCTOBER 4

Grow old along with me!
The best is yet to be,
The last of life, for which
The first was made.

—Robert Browning

OCTOBER 5

The man who makes it the habit of his life to go to bed at nine o'clock usually gets rich and is always reliable. Of course, going to bed does not make him rich—I merely mean that such a man will in all probability be up early in the morning and do a big day's work, so his weary bones put him to bed early. Honest men work by day. It's all a matter of habit, and good habits in America make any man rich. Wealth is largely a result of habit.

—John Jacob Astor

OCTOBER 6

The great rule of moral conduct is, next to God, to respect time.   *—Lavater*

OCTOBER 7

There's a time for some things and a time for all things; a time for great things and a time for small things.

—Cervantes

OCTOBER 8

No man can be provident of his time who is not provident in the choice of his company.   *—Jeremy Taylor*

OCTOBER 9

Time is cried upon as a great thief; it is people's own fault. Use him well, and you will get from his hand more than he will ever take from yours.   *—Miss Wetherell*

OCTOBER 10

Life and time are worth improving
Seize the moments while they stay
Seize and use them lest you lose them
And lament the wasted day.

—Sundial Inscription

OCTOBER 11

A man who gives his children habits of industry provides for them better than by giving them a fortune.

—Richard Whateley

OCTOBER 12

The future is purchased by the present.

—Samuel Johnson

October 13

Death, so called, is a thing which makes men weep
And yet a third of life is pass'd in sleep   —*Byron*

October 14

A man that is young in years may be old in hours, if he
hath lost no time.   —*Bacon*

October 15

Thou canst waste me; hold me back thou canst not.
     —*Sundial Inscription*

October 16

We live in deeds, not years; in thoughts, not breaths; in
feelings, not in figures on a dial; we should count time by
heart throbs. He most lives who thinks most, feels the
noblest, acts the best.   —*Philip James Bailey*

October 17

We have only one real concern in life—to live all the
time that fate allows us.   —*I. A. R. Wylie*

October 18

When ambition pulls one way, interest another, inclination a third, and perhaps reason contrary to all, a man is
likely to pass his time but ill who has so many different
parties to please. There is but one method of setting ourselves at rest in this particular, and that is adhering stead-
fastly to one great end as the chief and ultimate aim of all
our pursuits.   —*Addison*

OCTOBER 19

Be good, my dear, and let who will be clever
Do noble things, not dream them all day long
And so make life, death and the vast forever
One grand sweet song.

—*Charles Kingsley*

OCTOBER 20

The man who consecrates his hours
By vig'rous effort and an honest aim,
At once he draws the sting of life and death;
He walks with nature and her paths are peace.

—*Young*

OCTOBER 21

Who well lives, long lives; for this age of ours should not
be numbered by years, days and hours.   —*Du Bartas*

OCTOBER 22

None so little enjoy life and are such burdens to themselves as those who have nothing to do. The active only have the true relish of life.   —*G. Joy*

OCTOBER 23

Since life is short, we need to make it broad;
Since life is brief, we need to make it bright;
Then keep the old king's motto well in sight,
And let its meaning permeate each day
Whatever comes: "This, too, shall pass away."

—*Ella Wheeler Wilcox*

OCTOBER 24

"Had I not lived with Mirabeau," says Dumont, "I never should have known all that can be done in one day, or rather, in an interval of twelve hours. A day to him was of more value than a week or a month to others. Tomorrow was not to him the same impostor as to most others."

—Emerson

OCTOBER 25

The mill cannot grind with the water that is past.

—Sarah Doudney

OCTOBER 26

Age is opportunity no less
Than youth itself, though in another dress.

—Longfellow

OCTOBER 27

To show us the worth of time, God, most liberal of all other things, is exceedingly frugal in dispensing it; for He never gives us two moments together, nor grants us a second until He has withdrawn the first, still keeping the third in His own hands, so that we are in a perfect uncertainty whether we shall have it or not.   *—Fénelon*

OCTOBER 28

Many of us spend half our time wishing for things we could have if we did not spend half our time wishing.

—Alexander Woollcott

OCTOBER 29

Ah, nothing is too late
Until the tired heart shall cease to palpitate.
Cato learned Greek at eighty; Sophocles
Wrote his great Oedipus, and Simonides
Brought off the prize of verse from his compeers
When each had numbered more than four score years.

—Longfellow

OCTOBER 30

Who knows most, him loss of time most grieves.

—Dante

OCTOBER 31

Short as life is, we make it shorter by the careless waste
of time.   *—Victor Hugo*

NOVEMBER 1

Time is the one thing we possess. Our success depends
upon the use of our time, and its by-product, the odd
moment.   *—Arthur Brisbane*

NOVEMBER 2

To leave unseen so many a glorious sight
To leave so many lands unvisited
To leave so many worthiest books unread
Unrealized so many visions bright:
Oh! wretched yet inevitable spite
Of our brief span.

—Trench

November 3

Improve time in time,
While time lasts
All time is no time
When time is past.
—Townley Castle School Sundial

November 4

Very few men, properly speaking, live at present but are providing to live another time.   *—Swift*

November 5

To measure life learn thou betimes, and know
Towards solid good what leads the way.

—Milton

November 6

The difference between rising at five and seven in the morning, for the space of forty years, supposing a man to go to bed at the same hour at night, is nearly equivalent to the addition of ten years to a man's life.   *—Doddridge*

November 7

To be always intending to live a new life, but never to find time to set about it as if a man should put off eating and drinking and sleeping from one day and night to another, till he is starved and destroyed.   *—John Tillotson*

November 8

Do not refuse the employment which the hour brings you for one more ambitious.   *—Emerson*

November 9

We shall never have any more time. We have, and we have always had all the time there is. —*Arnold Bennett*

November 10

Most men eddy about
Here and there—eat and drink
Chatter and love and hate,
Gather and squander, are raised
Aloft, are hurl'd in the dust,
Striving blindly, achieving
Nothing, and then they die.

—*Matthew Arnold*

November 11

Next to temperance, a quiet conscience, a cheerful mind, and active habits, I place early rising as a means of health and happiness. —*Flint*

November 12

Today is the golden chance wherewith to snatch fruition;
There are asps among the figs;
For the potter's clay is in thy hands, to mould it or to mar
it at thy will,
Or idly to leave it in the sun, an uncouth lump to harden.

—*M. F. Tupper*

November 13

Consider that this day never dawns again. —*Dante*

November 14

Is there aught in sleep can charm the wise?
To lie in dead oblivion, losing half
The fleeting moments of too short a life;
Who would in such a gloomy state remain
Longer than nature craves?

—*Thomson*

November 15

Fill my hour, ye gods, so that I shall not say, whilst I have done this, "Behold, also, an hour of my life is gone," but rather, "I have lived an hour." —*Emerson*

November 16

Every day we unconsciously appraise life. And we appraise each day, each hour, in the same way. The proportion of our appreciation is measured by the valuation that we place upon these hours, days, months and on life itself.

—*George M. Adams*

November 17

Few ever lived to a great age, and fewer still ever became distinguished, who were not in the habit of early rising.

—*Dr. J. Todd*

November 18

The time God allots to each one of us is like a precious tissue which we embroider as best we know how.

—*Anatole France*

November 19

Time misspent is not lived, but lost.

—Dr. Thomas Fuller

November 20

For sluggard's brow the laurel never grows
Renown is not the child of indolent repose.

—Thomson

November 21

I do not think that seventy years is the time of a man or woman—nor that years will ever stop the existence of me, or any one else.   *—Walt Whitman*

November 22

In the midst of hope and care, in the midst of fears and disquietudes, think every day that shines upon you is the last. Thus the hour, which shall not be expected, will come upon you as an agreeable addition.   *—Horace*

November 23

By the street of "By and By" one arrives at the house of "Never."   *—Cervantes*

November 24

Know the true value of time; snatch, seize and enjoy every moment of it. No idleness; no laziness; no procrastination; never put off till tomorrow what you can do today.

—Lord Chesterfield

November 25

The present, the present, is all thou hast
For thy sure possession;
Let the patriarch's angel hold it fast
Till it gives its blessing.

—Whittier

November 26

Thus would I double my life's fading space
For he that runs it well runs twice his race.

—Abraham Cowley

November 27

Then be it yours, while you pursue
The golden moments, quick to haste
Some noble work of love to do,
Nor suffer one bright hour to waste.

—Colesworthy

November 28

True worth is in being, not seeming—
In doing each day that goes by
Some little good—not in dreaming
Of Great things to do by and by.

—Alice Cary

November 29

Nothing is ours but time.   *—Dr. Thomas Fuller*

November 30

The clock indicates the moment—but what does eternity
indicate?   *—Walt Whitman*

DECEMBER 1

Fill up each hour with what will last
Buy up the minutes as they go.

—Horatius Bonar

DECEMBER 2

The tissue of the Life to be
We weave with colors all our own
And in the field of Destiny
We reap as we have sown.

—Whittier

DECEMBER 3

Know'st thou yesterday, its aim and reason?
Work'st thou well today for worthier things?
Then calmly wait the morrow's hidden season
And fear thou not what hap so-e'er it brings.

—Goethe

DECEMBER 4

To be at work, to do things for the world, to turn the
currents of the things about us at our will, to make our
existence a positive element, even though it be no bigger
than a grain of sand—that is a new joy of which the idle
man knows no more than the mole knows of the sunshine,
nor the serpent of the eagle's triumphant flight into the
upper air.

—Phillips Brooks

DECEMBER 5

For all the frittered days
That I have spent in shapeless ways,—
Give me a perfect thing.

—Anna Wickham

DECEMBER 6

One ought, every day, at least to hear a little song, read
a good poem, see a fine picture, and, if it were possible,
to speak a few reasonable words.   *—Goethe*

DECEMBER 7

All things come to him who waits—provided he knows
what he is waiting for.   *—Woodrow Wilson*

DECEMBER 8

The heights by great men reached and kept
Were not attained by sudden flight
But they, while their companions slept,
Were toiling upward in the night.

—Longfellow

DECEMBER 9

The situation that has not its duty, its ideal, was never yet
occupied by man. Yes, here in this poor, miserable,
hampered, despicable Actual, wherein thou even now
standest—here or nowhere is thy ideal: work it out there-
from, and working, believe, live, be free!   *—Carlyle*

DECEMBER 10

Think naught a trifle though it small appear,
Small sands the mountain, moments make the year.

—Young

DECEMBER 11

The short period of life is long enough for living well and honorably.   *—Cicero*

DECEMBER 12

Well arranged time is the surest mark of a well arranged mind.   *—Pitman*

DECEMBER 13

Today is ours only
Work, work while you may;
There is no tomorrow
But only today.

—Luella Clark

DECEMBER 14

One by one the sands are flowing
One by one the moments fall;
Some are coming, some are going;
Do not strive to grasp them all.

—Adelaide Anne Procter

DECEMBER 15

We know nothing of tomorrow; our business is to be good and happy today.   *—Coleridge*

DECEMBER 16

He only can enrich me who can recommend to me the space between sun and sun. 'Tis the measure of a man—his apprehension of a day. —*Emerson*

DECEMBER 17

There are no fragments as precious as those of time, and none are so heedlessly lost by people who cannot make a moment, and yet can waste years. —*Robert Montgomery*

DECEMBER 18

The best preparation for tomorrow's work is to do your work as well as you can today. —*Elbert Hubbard*

DECEMBER 19

What is time?—the shadow on the dial—the striking of the clock,—the running of the sand, day and night,—summer and winter—months, years, centuries? These are but arbitrary and outward signs—the measure of time, not time itself. Time is the life of the soul. If not this then tell me what is time? —*Longfellow*

DECEMBER 20

Shun such as lounge through afternoons and eves;
And on thy dial write: "Beware of thieves!"
Felon of minutes, never taught to feel
The worth of treasures which thy fingers steal
Pick my left pocket of its silver dime
But spare the right, it holds my golden time!
—*Oliver Wendell Holmes*

DECEMBER 21

Lost wealth may be restored by industry—the wreck of health gained by temperance—forgotten knowledge restored by study—alienated friendship smoothed into forgetfulness —even forfeited reputation won by penitence and virtue. But who ever looked upon his vanished hours,—recalled his slighted years—stamped them with wisdom—or effaced from Heaven's record the fearful blot of wasted time?

—Mrs. Lydia H. Sigourney

DECEMBER 22

Observe a method in the distribution of your time. Every hour will then know its proper employment, and no time will be lost.   *—Bishop Horne*

DECEMBER 23

We ask for long life but it is deep life, or grand moments, that signify.   *—Emerson*

DECEMBER 24

The keen spirit
Seizes the prompt occasion—makes the thought
Start into instant action, and at once
Plans and performs, resolves and executes.

—Hannah More

DECEMBER 25

Do not think it wasted time to submit yourself to any influence that will bring upon you any noble feeling.

—Ruskin

DECEMBER 26

"I haven't time," I'm prone to say
But when I analyze my day
I find it is no shorter than
The day of any other man.
No man has more than I of time,
And if I let this gift sublime
Unfilled, stream into yesterday,
The time is lost, life thrown away.

—Anonymous

DECEMBER 27

There is room in human life to crowd almost every art and science in it. The more we do, the more we can do; the more busy we are, the more leisure we have.   *—Hazlitt*

DECEMBER 28

One of these days is none of these days.   *—Old Proverb*

DECEMBER 29

Cease to inquire what the future has in store, and take as a gift whatever the day brings forth.   *—Horace*

DECEMBER 30

Write it on your heart that every day is the best day of the year.   *—Emerson*

DECEMBER 31

It is vain to be always looking toward the future and never acting toward it.   *—Boyes*

INDEX TO AUTHORS QUOTED
IN TIME-THRIFT CALENDAR

147